UNBREAKABLE COURAGE

STRONG FAITH IN AN AGE OF ANXIETY, CHAOS, AND EXHAUSTION

BIBLE STUDY GUIDE

MAX LUCADO
WITH SAM O'NEAL

HarperChristian Resources

Unbreakable Courage Bible Study Guide

Published by HarperChristian Resources, 3950 Sparks Drive SE, Suite 101, Grand Rapids, MI 49546, USA. HarperChristian Resources is a registered trademark of HarperCollins Christian Publishing, Inc.

Requests for information should be addressed to customercare@harpercollins.com.

ISBN 978-0-310-17118-8 (softcover)
ISBN 978-0-310-17119-5 (ebook)

Published in association with Anvil II Management.

HarperChristian Resources titles may be purchased in bulk for church, business, fundraising, or ministry use. For information, please email ResourceSpecialist@ChurchSource.com.

HarperCollins Publishers, Macken House, 39/40 Mayor Street Upper, Dublin 1, D01 C9W8, Ireland (https://www.harpercollins.com).

Art direction: Ron Huizinga
Cover Design: © 2026 HarperCollins Christian Publishing
Interior Design: Inside Out Design

First Printing July 2026 / Printed in the United States of America

CONTENTS

SESSION 5: DON'T KISS THE SNAKE

SESSION 6: WAITING ON THE WHIRLWIND

A NOTE FROM MAX

Picture the scene. It's the dawn of a new day. The sun's light slowly illuminates the landscape. As shadows are cast aside, figures come into view. Crowds of thousands are making their way to the base of a mountain. They are coming from all across Israel—gaunt and thin from the dry spell on the land. They are curious about what the day will bring.

The minutes tick by, and other figures appear. The entrance of one man, presumably a king, causes a commotion. His henchmen clear a path and escort him to a place of prominence. He is followed by some 850 other notable figures, all dressed in robes and wearing religious ornaments. "The prophets," the people say. They cheer for them.

Then a murmur is heard among the crowd. A lone figure comes into view. He strides up the slope of the mountain, stops at the top, and leans on his staff. He stands opposite the 850 prophets . . . glaring at them. As you look on, it becomes clear the odds are against the fellow. He is outnumbered, outdone, and outgunned.

Who is this solitary figure? None other than the prophet Elijah. In his day, the spiritual condition in the kingdom of Israel was bleak. Elijah worshiped Yahweh, the one true God. Nearly all the Israelites did *not.* Rather, they worshiped gods named Baal and Asherah.

Elijah called those gods a hoax. He even went so far as to call for a showdown between these Canaanite gods and Yahweh to prove who truly had the power. Elijah issued this challenge to Ahab, the king of Israel, who took the bait. Ahab summoned 450 prophets of Baal and 400 prophets of Asherah to battle it out at Mount Carmel.

Now, at this point you might be asking what in the world Elijah's world has to do with you. Why spend six weeks diving into the life and times of a man who lived some 2,900 years in the past? Glad you asked. Elijah's story is relevant because the challenges he faced in his day are similar to the ones you face today.

Just like you, Elijah sought to honor God in a culture that was bent on dishonoring the Lord at every turn. Just like you, the odds were stacked against him, leaving him outnumbered and outgunned. And just like you, he often felt alone, anxious, and discouraged . . . becoming so downhearted at one point that he even pondered his own demise.

Yet just like you, Elijah wasn't alone. He was tethered to the Rock of Ages and empowered by the very Spirit of God. For that reason, he could remain steadfast in his faith and committed in maintaining his stand for God—even though his primary opponents were an evil king named Ahab and an even evil-er queen named Jezebel.

Elijah's courage was unbreakable not because he trusted in his own abilities but because he trusted in God. By studying his story, you can learn how to follow his example of unbreakable courage and unflinching faith. So . . . are you ready to begin?

— MAX LUCADO

HOW TO USE THIS BIBLE STUDY GUIDE

Nobody wants to be a coward. Nobody wants to be known as the one who runs away when the going gets tough. Nobody wants a reputation for being scared of their own shadow. No, we want to be brave! We want to face our foes and cry out, "Once more unto the breach, dear friends!"[1] We want to be women and men who are willing to stand up for what is right, true, and God-honoring despite the cost. We want to be people of *unbreakable courage*.

This study will help you pursue that goal by exploring the life of Elijah. You will engage with the story of this Old Testament prophet and discover some key principles that apply to the battleground of your life today. With the Lord's help, you can gain the strength to face whatever life throws at you with the same kind of steadfast courage and faith.

Before you begin, keep in mind there are a few ways you can go through this material. You can experience this study with others in a group (such as a Bible study, Sunday school class, or any other small-group gathering), or you can choose to go through the content on your own. Either way, know that the videos for each session are available for you to view at any time by following the instructions that have been provided with this study guide.

GROUP STUDY

Each of the sessions in this study is divided into two parts: (1) a group study section and (2) a personal study section. The group study section provides a basic framework on how to open your time together, get the most out of the video content, and discuss the key ideas that were presented in the teaching. Each session includes the following:

- **Welcome:** A short opening note about the topic of the session for you to read on your own before you meet as a group.
- **Connect:** An icebreaker question to get you and your group members thinking about the topic and interacting with each other or a time for the group members to discuss insights from the prior week.
- **Watch:** An outline of the key points covered in each video teaching along with space for you to take notes as you watch each session.

- **Discuss:** Questions to help you and your group reflect on the teaching material presented and apply it to your lives.
- **Respond:** A short personal exercise to help reinforce the key ideas.
- **Close:** A brief set of prompts to help you and your group members take the next step in inviting Jesus to be active and present in your lives and a place to record prayer requests (and praises) for the week.

If you are doing this study in a group, make sure you have your own copy of the study guide so you can write down your thoughts, responses, and reflections—and so you have access to the videos via streaming. You will also want to have a copy of the book *Unbreakable Courage*, as reading it alongside this guide will provide you with deeper insights. (See the notes at the beginning of each group session and personal study section on which chapters of the book you should read before the next group session.)

Finally, keep these points in mind:

- **Facilitation:** If you are doing this study in a group, you will want to appoint someone to serve as a facilitator. This person will be responsible for starting the video and keeping track of time during discussions and activities. If you have been chosen for this role, there are some resources in the back of this guide that can help you lead your group through the study.

- **Faithfulness:** Your group is a place where tremendous growth can happen as you reflect on the Bible, ask questions, and learn what God is doing in other people's lives. For this reason, be fully committed and attend each session so you can build trust and rapport with the other members.

- **Friendship:** The goal of any small group is to be a place where people can share, learn about God, and build friendships. So make your group a safe place. Be honest about your thoughts and feelings, but also listen carefully to everyone else's thoughts, feelings, and opinions. Keep anything personal that your group members share in confidence so that you can create a community where people can heal, be challenged, and grow spiritually.

If you are going through this study on your own, read the opening Welcome section and reflect on the questions in the Connect section. Watch the video and use the prompts provided to take notes. Personalize the questions and exercises in the Discuss and Respond sections. Close by recording any requests you want to pray about during the week.

PERSONAL STUDY

The personal study is for you to work through on your own during the week. Each exercise is designed to help you explore the key ideas you uncovered during your group time and delve into passages from the Bible that will help you apply those principles to your life. Go at your own pace, doing a little each day—or tackle the material all at once. Remember to spend a few moments in silence to listen to whatever God might be saying to you.

If you are doing this study as part of a group and are unable to finish (or even start) these personal studies for the week, still attend the group time. Be assured you are still wanted and welcome even if you don't have your "homework" done. These personal studies are merely intended to help you *hear* what God wants you to hear and *apply* what he is saying to your life. So, as you go through the material, listen for him to speak to you about what it means to develop strong faith in a world packed with anxiety, chaos, and exhaustion.

WEEK 1 *at a Glance*

THIS WEEK'S READING	Chapters 1–2 in *Unbreakable Courage*
GROUP MEETING	Read the Welcome and Connect with the group (page 3) Watch the video and take notes (pages 4–5) Discuss the questions that follow (page 6) Respond to the teaching and Close (pages 7–8)
PERSONAL STUDIES: Study 1 Study 2 Study 3	 "A Downward Spiral" (pages 10–13) "A Win in the Wilderness" (pages 14–17) "Pruning Away Pride" (pages 18–20)
CATCH UP AND READ AHEAD (BEFORE WEEK 2 MEETING)	Connect with someone in your group Complete any unfinished personal studies (page 21)
NEXT WEEK'S READING	Chapters 3–4 in *Unbreakable Courage*

SESSION ONE

GOD'S DIVINE BOOT CAMP

In the thirty-eighth year of Asa king of Judah, Ahab son of Omri became king of Israel, and he reigned in Samaria over Israel twenty-two years. Ahab son of Omri did more evil in the eyes of the LORD than any of those before him. . . . Now Elijah the Tishbite, from Tishbe in Gilead, said to Ahab, "As the LORD, the God of Israel, lives, whom I serve, there will be neither dew nor rain in the next few years except at my word."

1 KINGS 16:29-30; 17:1

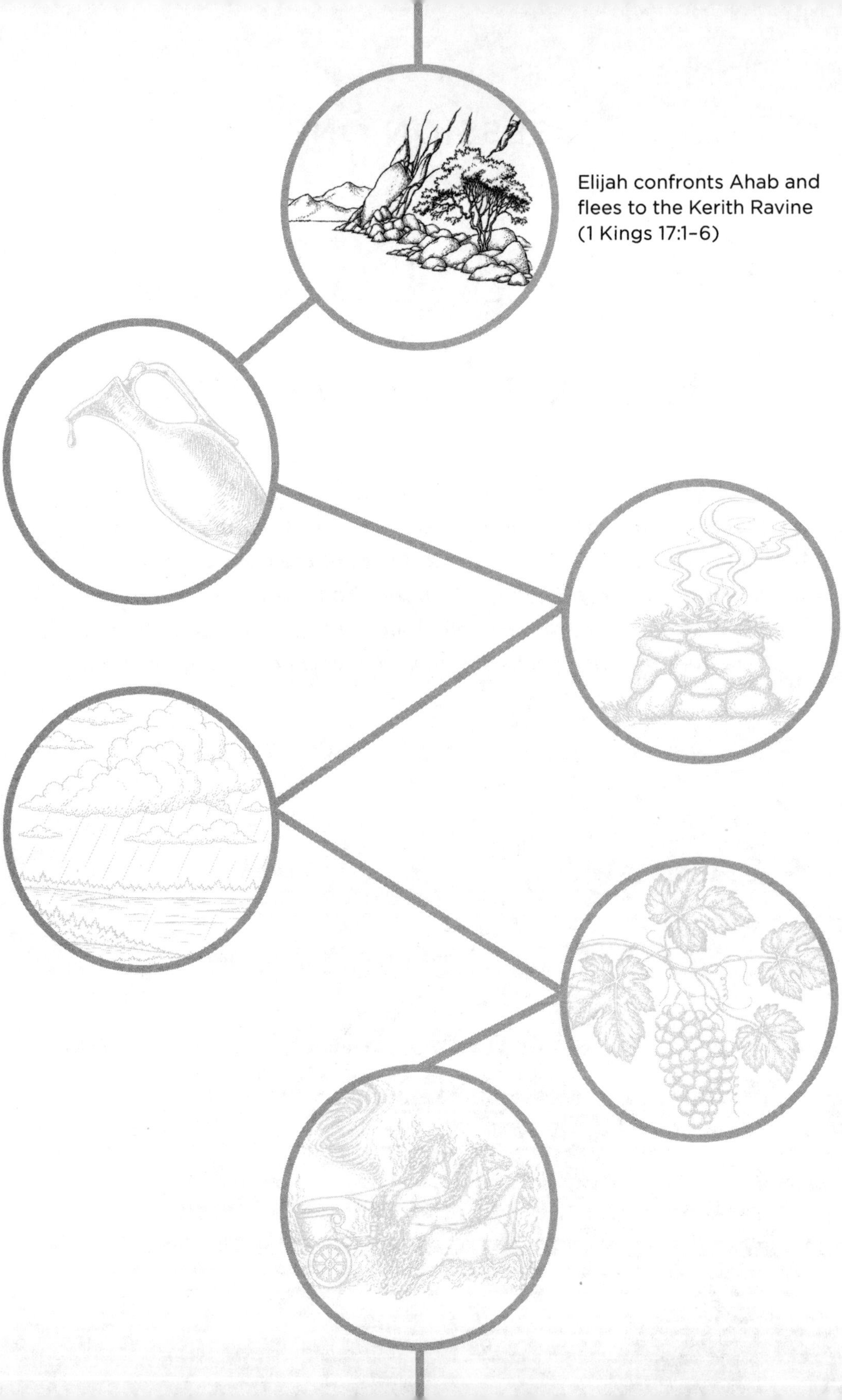
Elijah confronts Ahab and flees to the Kerith Ravine (1 Kings 17:1–6)

WELCOME | READ ON YOUR OWN

The first stop for anyone who wants to join the military is typically *boot camp.* If you were to visit such a camp, you would likely see soldiers marching in ranks, then dropping to the ground for round after round of push-ups. You'd hear the staccato burst of weapons fire and sergeants barking invectives at the top of their lungs. Your nose would be filled with the unpleasant scents of smoke and sweat and socks and . . . well, boots.

Take it all together, and you would come to the logical conclusion that boot camps are not places of pleasant pampering. They're not day spas. No, they're all about *preparation.*

Those who find themselves in boot camps receive basic training in important combat skills. This training is designed to transform civilians into service members. New recruits spend their days working long and hard hours and are exhausted when they hop into their bunks each night. They drill, drill, and drill some more so that one day, when they find themselves in a difficult or dangerous situation, they will react with confidence and skill.

Boot camps prepare people for action.

In this session, you will be introduced to the human "hero" of this study—a prophet named Elijah. But remember that heroes don't become heroes overnight. It requires preparation. This is why one of the first things you read about Elijah is that he spent several years alone by an insignificant brook in the middle of the wilderness. He didn't interact with people during that time but received all his food from a friendly flock of ravens.

As you can imagine, this was a trying time for Elijah. It was a season spent in God's divine boot camp. But it was also an important period of preparation so that Elijah would be ready for anything and everything that was to come.

CONNECT | 10 MINUTES

If you or any of your group members don't know each other, take a few minutes to introduce yourselves. Then choose one of the following questions to begin your discussion:

- Why did you decide to join this study? What do you hope to learn?

— *or* —

- What are some stories (fictional or historical) that have played a role in you becoming the person you are today?

WATCH | 25 MINUTES

Watch the video for this session, which you can access through streaming (see the instructions provided with this guide). Below is an outline of the key points covered during the teaching. Record any key concepts that stand out to you.

OUTLINE

I. Elijah could relate to feeling outnumbered and overwhelmed by the culture.

A. Elijah ministered in Israel during many decades of morally corrupt leadership.

B. The main purveyors of corruption in Elijah's day were Ahab and Jezebel.

C. Jezebel was especially involved with Baal worship and other forms of idolatry.

D. The wickedness of Israel's people (from the leaders down) did not escape God's notice.

II. Elijah burst onto the scene by proclaiming a drought in the land.

A. The physical conditions of this drought matched the spiritual dryness in Israel.

B. Elijah's promise of a drought was grounded in God's promises of what would happen if his people chose to worship other gods (see Deuteronomy 11:16–17).

C. The drought was a confrontation of Baal, who was connected with rain and fertility.

III. After this confrontation, God sent Elijah to an isolated place called the Kerith Ravine.

A. In that place Elijah was *cut off* from society and *cut down* in humility.

B. God sent Elijah to the wilderness to protect him and prepare him for the future.

C. God needed a steadfast prophet who could stand against a corrupt culture.

D. Even Jesus needed "Kerith-like" seasons of preparation (see Luke 4:1–13).

IV. Embrace seasons of solitude or isolation as part of God's divine boot camp.

A. These seasons teach us what it means to walk in the Spirit and how to lean on him as our Comforter.

B. It is in solitude that we find time to listen for God's voice and enjoy his presence.

C. Solitude reminds us that we cannot give out until we first take in.

D. The smaller we make ourselves, the more room we create for God to reveal his greatness to us.

NOTES

DISCUSS | 35 MINUTES

Discuss what you just watched by answering the following questions.

1. The culture of Elijah's day was notably immoral, in part because the king and queen promoted Baal worship and other forms of idolatry. When are some times that you felt pressured by modern culture to move away from God's values and priorities?

2. Elijah's statement to King Ahab was bold: "There will be neither dew nor rain in the next few years except at my word" (1 Kings 17:1). But that proclamation was rooted in God's promises from Scripture, including Deuteronomy 11:13–17. What might be some reasons why the Israelites failed to take those promises from God seriously?

3. Ask someone to read 1 Kings 17:2–6. Elijah was hidden from King Ahab in the Kerith Ravine but also isolated from his people. What are some seasons of loneliness or solitude you've endured in the past? What lessons did you learn from those seasons?

4. Instead of resisting seasons of isolation, it is possible to embrace them as opportunities to recognize God's closeness and provision in your life. When you feel cut off from others, what practical steps do you take to seek God for your needs?

5. Ask someone to read James 1:2–4. Boot camps are uncomfortable—even painful—yet serve an important purpose. What does James say about the purpose of facing trials? As a follower of Jesus, how might you retrain yourself to embrace the hard seasons of spiritual basic training rather than long for the comfortable spiritual "spa days"?

RESPOND | 10 MINUTES

God commanded Elijah to endure a season of solitude in the Kerith Ravine so he would be prepared for his future work. God needed a steadfast prophet who would stand against the tide of a corrupt culture, which meant Elijah needed to grow comfortable in isolation and in humility. But did you know that God himself followed a similar program of solitude and preparation when he walked the hills and valleys surrounding Jerusalem?

The first chapter of Mark describes the beginning of Jesus' public ministry in Galilee. He started by calling several disciples to follow him. Then he taught in the synagogue in Capernaum and cast out an unclean spirit. Then he healed Peter's mother-in-law of a high fever. Then he healed many other people and cast out demons. The Bible says the whole city was "gathered at the door" (Mark 1:33). Everyone wanted to see this incredible new rabbi!

You might think this would have been a great time for Jesus to establish a home base for his ministry. An opportunity for him to lean in to his public popularity and demonstrate even more miracles from God. But instead, look at what Jesus did next:

> [35] Very early in the morning, while it was still dark, Jesus got up, left the house and went off to a solitary place, where he prayed. [36] Simon and his companions went to look for him, [37] and when they found him, they exclaimed: "Everyone is looking for you!" [38] Jesus replied, "Let us go somewhere else—to the nearby villages—so I can preach there also. That is why I have come."
>
> MARK 1:35-38

Jesus sought moments of solitude to connect with the Father. How are you currently incorporating similar moments of solitude and connection in your daily routine?

Do you feel like your current spiritual walk provides time and space for God to prepare you for the work he wants you to accomplish each day? Explain your response.

CLOSE | 10 MINUTES

When the time comes to close this session, talk with God about the many ways he has prepared and equipped you to be servants in his kingdom—including seasons of solitude. Express gratitude for those seasons and for the ways God has preserved you and provided for you in the midst of them. Commit to actively making time for God to fill you each day so you have something to give at home, at work, and beyond. Use the space below to write down any requests so you and your group members can pray about them in the week ahead.

Name	Request

SESSION ONE

PERSONAL STUDY

It is likely that you have come to this study because you want strong faith in an age of anxiety, chaos, and exhaustion. Like Elijah, you desire to be a person of unbreakable courage who stands for what is right no matter how hard the culture around you pushes you to conform. To help you accomplish those goals, the personal study section in each session will offer you a deeper look at passages from the Bible and give you some solid principles you can incorporate into your daily effort to stand. If you are doing this study with a group, make sure to write down your responses to the questions, as you will be given a few minutes to share your insights at the start of the next session. If you are reading *Unbreakable Courage* alongside this study, you may want to first review chapters 1–2 of the book.

STUDY 1

A DOWNWARD SPIRAL

Context is important when studying Scripture, so let's take a step back and gain some perspective on where Elijah's story fits in the larger story of the Old Testament. As you might recall, the nation of Israel was split in two after King Solomon died. The southern portion of the nation was renamed Judah and ruled by Solomon's son Rehoboam, while the northern kingdom retained the name of Israel and was ruled by a king named Jeroboam.

Jeroboam was an idolater. He did not want his fellow Israelites journeying to Jerusalem every year to worship at the temple, so he created two golden calves in two separate cities and told the people to worship there instead. He even declared, "Here are your gods, Israel, who brought you up out of Egypt" (1 Kings 12:28).

Things went downhill from there. Consider the next five kings of Israel:

- Jeroboam's son Nadab took the reins (pun intended) from his father, but he didn't last long. A man named Baasha killed him and all his family.
- Baasha ruled for twenty-four years and maintained Jeroboam's idolatry.
- Baasha's son Elah was next. He survived only two years before a military general named Zimri killed him and tried to take the throne.
- Zimri lasted only seven days before Omri, commander of the entire army, came after him. Zimri, seeing that he would be defeated, burned down the king's palace with himself inside.
- Omri became king and ruled for twelve years. He pushed the people to worship idols, just as Jeroboam and Baasha had done before him.

Talk about a bad batch of kings! Even so, here is what the Bible says about Omri's son Ahab, who was next in line for the throne: "Ahab did more to provoke the LORD God of Israel to anger than all the kings of Israel who were before him" (1 Kings 16:33 NKJV).

Ahab was the king whom God called Elijah to confront—Ahab and his wicked wife, Jezebel. This cruel combo had murdered the priests and prophets of God while pampering the false priests of a false god named Baal. It was for this reason that God used his divine boot camp at the Kerith Ravine to harden and hone Elijah into a steadfast warrior of faith.

1. Read 1 Kings 12:25–33. Jeroboam, the first king of the northern tribes of Israel, led the people into the worship of two golden calves. In the decades that followed, the leaders of the northern kingdom continued to advocate for its people to worship idols. How do you imagine these leaders influenced the citizens who wanted to worship the Lord God alone?

2. Jeroboam was able to create a culture of idol worship in Israel. How much pressure do you feel to conform to culture when it comes to these forms of idolatry?

The idol of money and possessions

1	2	3	4	5	6	7	8	9	10
[a little]									[a lot]

The idol of fame and success

1	2	3	4	5	6	7	8	9	10
[a little]									[a lot]

The idol of power and influence

1	2	3	4	5	6	7	8	9	10
[a little]									[a lot]

The idol of comfort and ease

1	2	3	4	5	6	7	8	9	10
[a little]									[a lot]

The idol of ego and pride

1	2	3	4	5	6	7	8	9	10
[a little]									[a lot]

3. Idolatry in our culture doesn't typically involve religious temples or graven images, which makes it difficult to spot. How can you know whether something is an idol in our culture? How do you know whether something has become an idol in your life?

Winds of society whip us. Each day brings a new challenge. Turn this way, there is conflict. That way, there is tension. Look behind you and a posse of problems is coming after you. It's enough to make a person want to give up. Give up on God. Give up on the future. Give up on life.

Just give up.

Yet the story of Elijah offers us hope. It is a field manual on how to thrive during a spiritual drought. Elijah shows us that one person following a living God is greater than hundreds of people praying to a lifeless one. . . .

As much as any person in the Bible, Elijah affirms a positive answer to these questions: Can a person maintain faith in a world that has little? When a culture belittles belief, can a believer beget strength?

Yes![2]

4. Paul wrote, "Let us not become weary in doing good, for at the proper time we will reap a harvest if we do not give up" (Galatians 6:9). What are some of the things that "weary" you when it comes to doing good? What is the promise given to you in this verse if you don't give up?

> 16:31 [Ahab] not only considered it trivial to commit the sins of Jeroboam son of Nebat, but he also married Jezebel daughter of Ethbaal king of the Sidonians, and began to serve Baal and worship him. 32 He set up an altar for Baal in the temple of Baal that he built in Samaria. 33 Ahab also made an Asherah pole and did more to arouse the anger of the LORD, the God of Israel, than did all the kings of Israel before him. . . . 17:1 Now Elijah the Tishbite . . . said to Ahab, "As the LORD, the God of Israel, lives, whom I serve, there will be neither dew nor rain in the next few years except at my word."
>
> 1 KINGS 16:31–33; 17:1

5. Elijah's story begins with the Lord sending a *physical* drought on the land that matched the *spiritual* drought the people were experiencing. When have you experienced times of spiritual drought? How did God help you to thrive during those times?

6. Based on what you've read so far, why do you think God sent Elijah to Israel at this particular time in its history? What does this act reveal about God's nature?

STUDY 2

A WIN IN THE WILDERNESS

Elijah wasn't the only representative of God's kingdom who spent time in solitude before launching a successful ministry. Jesus himself sought out an isolated spot to be alone with God after his first day of confronting demons and healing the sick in Capernaum. As Mark writes in his Gospel, "Very early in the morning, while it was still dark, Jesus got up, left the house and went off to a solitary place, where he prayed" (1:35).

Luke provides us with a few details of how Jesus handled his season in the wilderness. Right after Jesus' encounter at the Jordan River with John the Baptist, but before his public ministry began, we read, "Jesus, full of the Holy Spirit, left the Jordan and was led by the Spirit into the wilderness, where for forty days he was tempted by the devil. He ate nothing during those days, and at the end of them he was hungry" (4:1–2).

Right away, we see a big difference between Jesus and Elijah. The prophet had food available to him. "The ravens brought him bread and meat in the morning and bread and meat in the evening, and he drank from the brook" (1 Kings 17:6). Jesus ate *nothing* for forty days. Worse than that, Jesus had to deal with Satan's harassment during his time of preparation. It was there in the wilderness that the devil tempted the Savior with promises of bread, kingdoms, and grandeur.

Of course, Jesus refused them all.

Right now you might be thinking, *What was the point of Jesus being in the wilderness? After all, he is the Son of God. Why did he need a boot camp?*

Jesus is more than the sacrificial Lamb who died for our sins. He is also the fulfillment of Adam—the perfect man who lived a perfect life in perfect obedience to the Father. "The first man was of the dust of the earth; the second man is of heaven"(1 Corinthians 15:47). Part of Jesus' obedience was total dependence on the Father for provision. Another part was Jesus being filled by the Father so that he could pour himself out for us.

In Jesus' own words, "Very truly I tell you, the Son can do nothing by himself; he can do only what he sees his Father doing, because whatever the Father does the Son also does. For the Father loves the Son and shows him all he does. Yes, and he will show him even greater works than these, so that you will be amazed" (John 5:19–20).

1. Read the story of the season that Jesus spent in the wilderness in Matthew 4:1–11. When have you experienced a season when you felt cut off from important resources or from important people in your life? How did that season help you grow?

2. Jesus not only spent time in God's boot camp *before* the start of his ministry but also retreated *during* his ministry to spend time with his Father. Look up the following passages and record what happened immediately after Jesus spent these times in prayer.

Luke 4:42–44

Luke 6:12–16

Luke 9:18–20

3. God directed Elijah to an isolated brook and "directed the ravens" to supply him with food in the wilderness (1 Kings 17:4). Why do you think God chose to provide for Elijah's needs in this way? What might the Lord have been teaching his prophet?

> Strength develops in Kerith. Do not resist the season of isolation; embrace it. Turn to God as your best friend. . . . Explore the benefits of silence. Take advantage of the small sabbaticals that come your way: the early morning moments, the time in the car as you commute, the minutes before you board a plane.
>
> Lay claim to a quiet place, a spot where you can hear God's voice and where you can be honest with self and God. Nothing to lose, gain, or conceal. A park, closet, or patio. Make regular visits for the singular purpose of being alone with God. Speak less when you are in his presence. Let your words be precise and few, not vague and many. Learn to savor the stillness. Trust God's stops as well as God's steps.
>
> It can be good to be cut off for a time. We cannot give out unless we learn to take in.[3]

4. Elijah had plenty of time to explore the benefits of solitude in the Kerith Ravine. Look at some of the benefits this kind of solitude offers you in the above quote, and then underline any suggestions you would like to try this week. What would it take for you to actually do this? What priorities would you need to shift to make it happen?

5. One of the reasons you *need* time alone with God is so he can fill you up with resources that you then pour out to others. In what areas of life do you feel depleted right now—even empty? What would it look like for God to fill you up in those areas?

> 4 "Abide in Me, and I in you. As the branch cannot bear fruit of itself, unless it abides in the vine, neither can you, unless you abide in Me.
>
> 5 "I am the vine, you are the branches. He who abides in Me, and I in him, bears much fruit; for without Me you can do nothing. 6 If anyone does not abide in Me, he is cast out as a branch and is withered; and they gather them and throw them into the fire, and they are burned. 7 If you abide in Me, and My words abide in you, you will ask what you desire, and it shall be done for you. 8 By this My Father is glorified, that you bear much fruit; so you will be My disciples."
>
> JOHN 15:4-8 NKJV

6. We live in a society of abundant supply. Whatever material things we need—food, clothing, technology—can be purchased and delivered in hours. How do you reconcile that reality with the truth expressed by Jesus in this passage? What do you think Jesus is asking you to do when he invites you to "abide" in him?

STUDY 3

PRUNING AWAY PRIDE

There is a good chance that one of the reasons God enrolled Elijah in his divine boot camp was to take him down a peg or two in terms of pride. When you look at how Elijah burst into Ahab's throne room to make his dramatic proclamation, it's clear he didn't lack confidence. The prophet was no shrinking violet. But God knew the road Elijah would need to walk in the coming years, so he determined to equip him with an extra measure of humility.

We will see why Elijah needed that humility as we continue through his story in the sessions to come. But for now, let's look at another bold and brash believer in the Bible who needed his Master to trim his hat size a little before he could truly be ready to serve. Who is this figure? None other than the apostle Peter.

Matthew records a moment in his Gospel that started out as a moment of triumph for Peter. When Jesus gathered his disciples together and asked, "Who do you say I am?" Peter was ready with the answer: "You are the Messiah, the Son of the living God" (16:15–16).

Big points for Peter! Jesus commended him, saying, "Blessed are you, Simon son of Jonah, for this was not revealed to you by flesh and blood, but by my Father in heaven. And I tell you that you are Peter, and on this rock I will build my church, and the gates of Hades will not overcome it" (verses 17–18).

What a moment. With a single confession of truth, Peter was launched to the head of the class. The Savior called him a "rock."

But things got rockier just a few verses later.

Matthew writes, "From that time on Jesus began to explain to his disciples that he must go to Jerusalem and suffer many things at the hands of the elders, the chief priests and the teachers of the law" (verse 21). But Peter didn't like that kind of talk. Perhaps, now that he was "top dog," he thought he should give Jesus a little check. After all, the Messiah was lowering morale with all this talk of death.

"Peter took him aside and began to rebuke him. 'Never, Lord!' he said. 'This shall never happen to you!'" (verse 22). As you might imagine, Jesus moved quickly to prune Peter's pride: "But He turned and said to Peter, 'Get behind Me, Satan! You are an offense to Me, for you are not mindful of the things of God, but the things of men'" (verse 23 NKJV).

1. Read the entire story of Jesus and Peter's interaction in Matthew 16:13–23. Jesus called Peter both a "rock" and a "stumbling block." How could both be true at the same time?

2. Read the rest of Jesus' words to Peter (and the other disciples) in Matthew 16:24–27. What does Jesus say about what it truly means to be his disciple? What does Jesus say is the ultimate reward for his true followers?

> 5 You who are younger, submit yourselves to your elders. All of you, clothe yourselves with humility toward one another, because,
>
> "God opposes the proud
> but shows favor to the humble."
>
> 6 Humble yourselves, therefore, under God's mighty hand, that he may lift you up in due time. 7 Cast all your anxiety on him because he cares for you.
>
> 1 PETER 5:5-7

3. Peter wrote the words above, which shows that he had learned a thing or two about the value of humility. What does it mean to "clothe" yourself with humility? What are some practical steps you can take to make sure that happens in your life?

4. Think back to a time in recent weeks when you had an opportunity to demonstrate humility—to make yourself low rather than lift yourself up high. How did you respond in that moment? What would you change about your response in hindsight?

The enemy of the saint is pride. We must fight it like the foe it is. My friend Rick Atchley says, "If you are too big to do something small, you are too small to do something big."[4]

Take note of your "hat size." Are you getting a big head? Then volunteer for menial tasks. Wash dishes. Sweep floors. Take a page from the successful recording artist Rich Mullins, who was known to duck away from lavish awards banquets only to pop up in a catering uniform to serve others.[5]

You are loved but not indispensable. You are God's child but not God's golden child. You have a place in God's plan, but you are not essential to God's plan. The smaller we are, the more room there is for God.[6]

5. "We must fight [pride] like the foe it is." In your life, how do you fight the impulse to be prideful? What has worked for you? What hasn't worked—and why?

6. Jesus established the model for humility when he said, "The Son of Man did not come to be served, but to serve, and to give his life as a ransom for many" (Mark 10:45). Why is serving others the antidote to pride? What are you currently doing to serve others?

CATCH UP AND READ AHEAD

Connect with a fellow group member this week and discuss some of the key insights from this session. Use any of the following prompts to help guide your discussion.

- What have you liked best from the content in this session, including both the group study and the personal study?
- Where do you feel pressured by the culture to indulge in idolatry? What steps are you currently taking to resist that idolatry?
- In what ways do you currently feel cut off from resources? What does it look like to intentionally seek God as the provider for those resources?
- Do you feel as if you are presently in God's boot camp? If so, what might God be using this time of preparation to enable you to do?
- What does it look like to help one another be aware of pride? How can you point out potential areas of danger without being offensive?

Use this time to go back and complete any of the study and reflection questions from previous days that you weren't able to finish. Make a note below of any revelations you've had and reflect on any growth or personal insights you've gained.

Read chapters 3–4 in *Unbreakable Courage* before the next group gathering. Use the space below to note anything in those chapters that stands out to you or encourages you.

WEEK 2 *at a Glance*

THIS WEEK'S READING	Chapters 3–4 in *Unbreakable Courage*
GROUP MEETING	Read the Welcome and Connect with the group (page 25) Watch the video and take notes (pages 26–27) Discuss the questions that follow (page 28) Respond to the teaching and Close (pages 29–30)
PERSONAL STUDIES: Study 1 Study 2 Study 3	 "Pray in Faith" (pages 32–35) "Pray with Persistence" (pages 36–39) "Pray with Confidence" (pages 40–44)
CATCH UP AND READ AHEAD (BEFORE WEEK 3 MEETING)	Connect with someone in your group Complete any unfinished personal studies (page 45)
NEXT WEEK'S READING	Chapters 5–6 in *Unbreakable Courage*

SESSION TWO

PRAY IT THROUGH

"As surely as the Lord *your God lives," [the widow] replied, "I don't have any bread—only a handful of flour in a jar and a little olive oil in a jug. I am gathering a few sticks to take home and make a meal for myself and my son, that we may eat it—and die." Elijah said to her, "Don't be afraid. Go home and do as you have said. But first make a small loaf of bread for me from what you have and bring it to me, and then make something for yourself and your son. For this is what the* Lord*, the God of Israel, says: 'The jar of flour will not be used up and the jug of oil will not run dry until the day the* Lord *sends rain on the land.'"*

1 KINGS 17:12-14

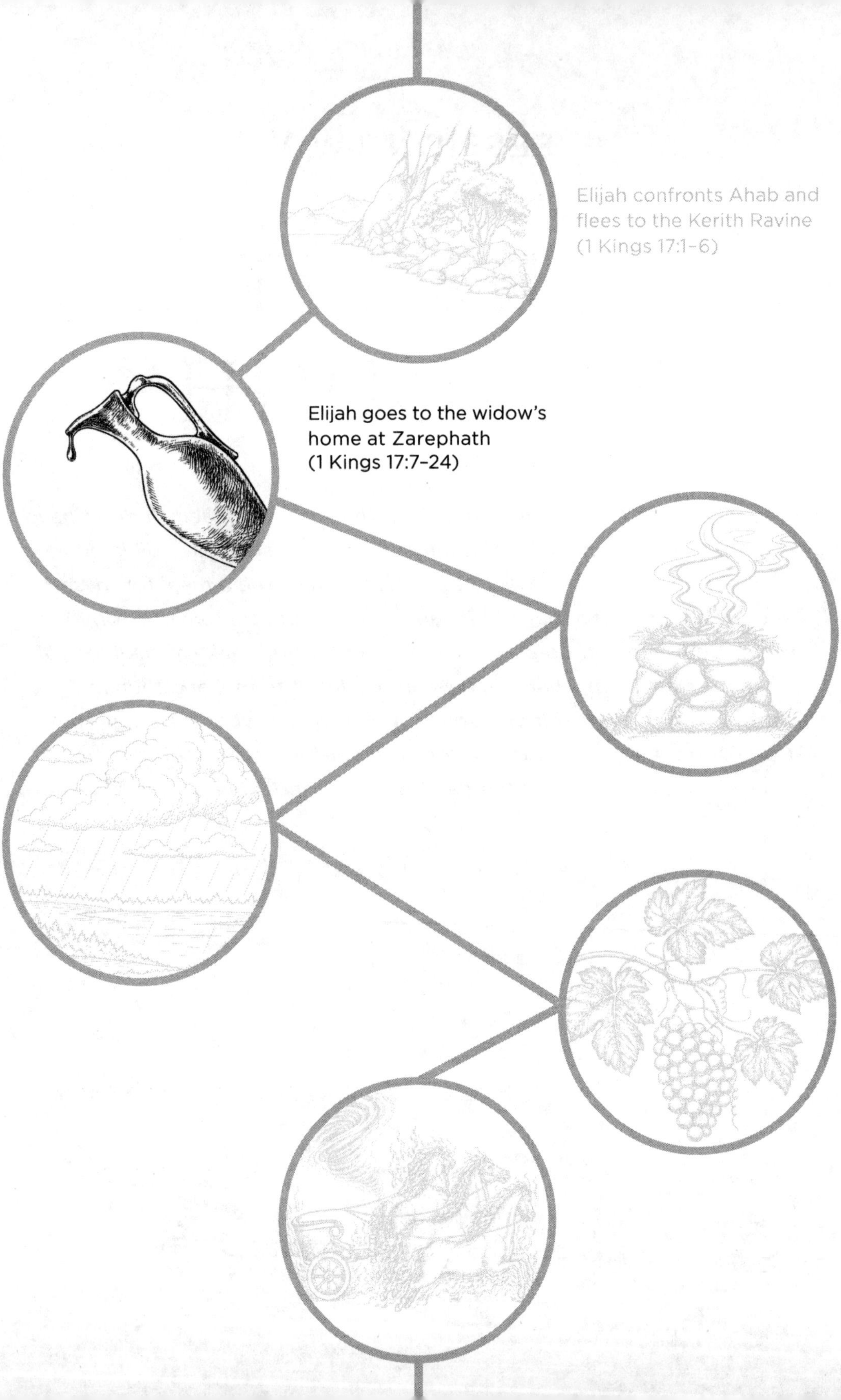
Elijah confronts Ahab and
flees to the Kerith Ravine
(1 Kings 17:1–6)
Elijah goes to the widow's
home at Zarephath
(1 Kings 17:7–24)

WELCOME | READ ON YOUR OWN

Back when you were a kid, you heard a lot of "make sure" statements from your parents and other adults in your life. "Make sure you brush your teeth." "Make sure you never take candy from strangers." "Make sure you look both ways before crossing the street."

These are things that kids generally know they are supposed to do, yet adults keep reminding about them anyway. Why? Because kids don't always do what they're supposed to do! If you are the parent of a child of any age, you know this is true. They make choices based on what feels best right now instead of what makes the most logical sense for the future.

There are some "make sure" statements that Christians hear often as well. "Make sure you go to church." "Make sure you read your Bible." "Make sure you pray each day." Once again, these are things that Christians know they are supposed to do as followers of Jesus. They understand, at least at an intellectual level, that such practices are important.

Still, knowing and doing aren't the same thing. Or, perhaps more accurately, knowing that you're supposed to do something isn't the same as doing it consistently and effectively.

This can be especially true for prayer. There are believers in Christ who genuinely want to be effective in prayer, but they're uncertain as to how to go about it. *Am I doing it right? Am I praying often enough or long enough? Should I be using some kind of outline or formula? Should I be hearing from God in a specific way?*

In this session, you will explore some of these themes as you continue in Elijah's story. You will see that the prophet made prayer his primary strategy in the midst of tragedy. Thankfully, he also offered several strategies that will help you to be more effective as you hit your knees in preparation for talking with God.

CONNECT | 10 MINUTES

If you or any of your group members don't know each other, take a few minutes to introduce yourselves. Then discuss one or both of the following questions.

- If you had to eat the same meal again and again for a week, what particular meal would you choose? Why?

— or —

- How do you typically feel when you prepare to approach God in prayer?

WATCH | 25 MINUTES

Now watch the video for this session. Below is an outline of the key points covered during the teaching. Record any key concepts that stand out to you.

OUTLINE

I. Elijah had gone from the throne room of Ahab to the wilderness at Kerith.

A. We can imagine it was fairly easy for Elijah to remain dependent on God when the brook was flowing and the ravens were bringing him food.

B. However, depending on God became more difficult when the brook dried up during the drought.

C. We tend to feel the same—it's easy to trust God when provision is already there.

II. Eventually, God sent Elijah to Zarephath, where a widow would provide for him.

A. This would not have instilled confidence in Elijah that he would soon be out of his situation.

B. The hundred-mile-long hike through the drylands would have posed a challenge.

C. Zarephath was governed by Baal worshipers—and Elijah was a wanted man.

D. To his credit, Elijah obeyed the will of the Lord and set out on the journey.

III. The widow in Zarephath was one drop away from empty herself.

A. The widow's resources consisted of a handful of flour and a tiny jug of olive oil.

B. Elijah could have given up, but he remembered how God had kept his promises.

C. Elijah was courageous and had faith that the Lord would provide for him, the widow, and her son.

D. The widow did as Elijah asked, and she received the blessing God had promised.

IV. Prayer was Elijah's strategy when the widow's child died sometime later.

A. The widow had witnessed God's provision, but when her son died, it seemed it had all been for nothing.

B. Like Moses before him, Elijah responded by wrestling with God in prayer.

C. Fervent prayer changes the one who prays—it's how Elijah became Elijah.

D. The power of "praying it through" was demonstrated when the son of the widow returned to life.

NOTES

DISCUSS | 35 MINUTES

Discuss what you just watched by answering the following questions.

1. At the Kerith Ravine, Elijah enjoyed a season of provision and then watched as the waters ran dry. Why do you think God allowed Elijah to feel the effects of the drought? What further training was God giving to Elijah in learning how to trust in him?

2. Ask someone to read 1 Kings 17:7–9. Zarephath was a center of Baal worship and—for good measure—the hometown of Jezebel. It seemed like a terrible place for a wanted man like Elijah to hide. What does it say about Elijah that he obeyed God anyway? When has God asked you to do something like this that at first did not make sense?

3. Elijah told the widow, "This is what the LORD, the God of Israel, says: 'The jar of flour will not be used up and the jug of oil will not run dry until the day the LORD sends rain on the land'" (1 Kings 17:14). What part do you think Elijah's remembrance of how God had just provided for his needs played in his making this pronouncement to the widow?

4. Ask someone to read Luke 11:9–10. The Greek verbs used in this passage imply continuous and repeated action: "*keep* asking," "*keep* seeking, "*keep* knocking." How did Elijah demonstrate persistence (and passion) in his prayers for the widow's son? What does his example say about the importance of fervent and faithful prayers?

5. Elijah wasn't the offspring of angels or embedded with spiritual superpowers at birth. He became great in God's kingdom because of his fervent prayers and courageous obedience. How does that truth inspire you today? If you were to pray an Elijah-level prayer today over a situation that you want to be resolved . . . what would you say?

RESPOND | 10 MINUTES

One of the reasons prayer can seem difficult is because we imagine needing to catch God's attention or attract his notice. We think of him as up in heaven managing the cosmos, which makes it intimidating to initiate contact—as if we're pestering or bothering him.

Sometimes we might be tempted to try to "earn" the access we need by using impressive words, passionate emotions, and even lots of volume. But here's the reality: God is more interested in us just *speaking* with him than he is in the *way* we choose to do it. Jesus made this clear when he gave this instruction in the Sermon on the Mount:

> 5 "And when you pray, do not be like the hypocrites, for they love to pray standing in the synagogues and on the street corners to be seen by others. Truly I tell you, they have received their reward in full. 6 But when you pray, go into your room, close the door and pray to your Father, who is unseen. Then your Father, who sees what is done in secret, will reward you. 7 And when you pray, do not keep on babbling like pagans, for they think they will be heard because of their many words. 8 Do not be like them, for your Father knows what you need before you ask him."
>
> MATTHEW 6:5-8

What type of attitude is Jesus addressing in this passage when it comes to prayer? What kind of heart does God want you to have when you approach him?

What does Jesus say about your ability to "catch" God's attention? When you think of God as a loving heavenly Father, how should that affect the way you pray?

CLOSE | 10 MINUTES

Conclude by taking a few moments to affirm the truth of God's Word that your heavenly Father has his ears open to your prayers. Thank him for the opportunity to pray at any moment about anything. Ask for the discipline and strength necessary to stand against the enemy by falling on your knees. Use the space below to write down any requests from the group so you can put this into practice during the week and intercede for each other!

Name	Request

SESSION TWO

PERSONAL STUDY

The more you read Elijah's story, the more similarities you find with your own. As you saw in the first session, there will be times when God puts you through his divine boot camp. He will do this to prepare you for the mission ahead and will sustain you during this time. But there will also be times when God orchestrates events to move you to the next stage in his plan. The brook runs dry . . . and he asks you to move on to your own version of Zarephath. Prayer becomes real at these times—a survival tool when the situation is bleak and courage is needed. In this personal study, you will consider the role of faith in your prayers, how to be persistent in prayer, and how to take the "corpses" of your life and lay them before the Lord. Continue to write down your responses to share with the group, and if you are reading *Unbreakable Courage* alongside this study, first review chapters 3–4 of the book.

STUDY 1

PRAY IN FAITH

Faith is a key element in the story of Elijah. The prophet didn't just believe that God was real. He believed that what God said was true. More than that, Elijah took bold action based on that belief.

When Elijah confronted Ahab and Jezebel, he did so at the risk of his own life. Baal was a Canaanite god known by epithets such as "rider of the clouds." He was associated with rain, lightning, wind, and fertility.[7] Elijah, in announcing that God would bring a drought, was proclaiming Baal to be powerless over the very thing he was supposed to hold power over! This made Elijah a hated and hunted enemy of the state.

Even so, Elijah continued to act in faith. When God sent him to the Kerith, he went. When God sent him to a widow in Zarephath, he traveled a hundred miles to seek her out.

One of the reasons you need faith to follow God is that God often gives his people what seem like baffling commands. Just think about Joshua, who followed in Moses' footsteps. Joshua was charged with leading the Israelite army into the promised land. But when the Israelite forces reached the first city of Jericho, the Lord told them not to attack. Instead, he commanded Joshua to lead the people in a march around the city for six days and then—on the seventh day—to march around the city seven times and blow a bunch of trumpets and shout really loud. How were shouts supposed to defeat stone?

Or think about Gideon, a leader in Israel during the time of the judges. The Lord commanded Gideon to attack the Midianites, who were causing all kinds of trouble for God's people. But the Lord commanded Gideon to do this with just three hundred soldiers. How was an army that outnumbered supposed to defeat the enemy?

Or think about poor Martha, the sister of Mary and Lazarus, who waited four days for Jesus to show up. By the time the Savior arrived, her brother had already died. But then she heard Jesus instruct for the stone to be rolled away from the tomb. What was Jesus hoping to accomplish—other than making the bystanders nauseated at the stench of the decaying body?

None of those commands made sense. But each led to incredible acts of God's power. It just took faith. So it is that when we kneel before the throne of God, we believe not only that he *exists* but that he has the power to move in our lives. We believe that what he has promised is true. And we are ready and willing to take action on that belief, as Elijah did

1. A dictionary definition of *faith* is "a firm belief in something for which there is no proof." For example, "They had *faith* that everything would work out."[8] But this is not exactly the biblical definition of faith. When you consider Elijah's story, what "proof" did he have that God would come through for him? How did that influence his faith?

2. A biblical definition of faith is found in Hebrews 11:1: "Faith is confidence in what we hope for and assurance about what we do not see." Notice the two aspects in this definition: (1) confident hope in God, and (2) assurance about what we don't see.

Think about this definition. What confident hope do you have in God today?

What gives you assurance that your trust in God is well-founded?

What does it look like to pray in a way that demonstrates your faith?

What does it look like to pray in a way that is saturated with faith?

3. Elijah's pronouncement of the drought came with consequences. Obadiah, a palace administrator, later told him, "There is not a nation or kingdom where my master has not sent someone to look for you" (1 Kings 18:10). What does Elijah's willingness to act in spite of the risks say about his faith? What does this say about the kind of courage that is often required to step up and act in faith?

13 Is anyone among you in trouble? Let them pray. Is anyone happy? Let them sing songs of praise. 14 Is anyone among you sick? Let them call the elders of the church to pray over them and anoint them with oil in the name of the Lord. 15 And the prayer offered in faith will make the sick person well; the Lord will raise them up. If they have sinned, they will be forgiven. 16 Therefore confess your sins to each other and pray for each other so that you may be healed. The prayer of a righteous person is powerful and effective. 17 Elijah was a human being, even as we are. He prayed earnestly that it would not rain, and it did not rain on the land for three and a half years.

JAMES 5:13–17

4. What connection does James make in this passage between prayer and faith? What is the promise given to the person who offers up a prayer in faith?

5. Why does James use the example of Elijah as an example of faithful prayer? What is he stressing by saying that "Elijah was a human being, even as we are" (verse 17)?

If God gives the task, he will give the tools. God told the widow to feed the prophet and then gave her the resources to do so. "God is able to make all grace abound toward you, that you, always having all sufficiency in all things, may *have an abundance for every good work*" (2 Corinthians 9:8 NKJV).

God will give you what you need when you need it.

The widow had provisions adequate for one day, not two. He does the same today. We'd rather have it all at once. We'd prefer to fill a storehouse with a lifetime's worth of courage, cash, and convictions. But God wants us to trust him day by day, moment by moment.[9]

6. "If God gives the task, he will give the tools." Think about the tasks that God has given you to do. What are some of the resources you need to complete those tasks? What is your prayer of faith today that he will provide those needed resources to you?

STUDY 2

PRAY WITH PERSISTENCE

Wouldn't it be nice if there was a verse in the Bible guaranteeing that followers of Jesus would never struggle? Alas, the opposite is true. Scripture is stained with tears, problems, injustices, immorality, and wars. Tough times come with life. That's the bad news.

The good news is that troubling times don't have to take the life out of your life. That's because whatever is troubling you, you have the opportunity to pray it through.

What is *it*?

Whatever is troubling you, wringing you out, or dragging you down. *It* is the future that seems to be spiraling out of control—dissolving all your well-laid plans into dust. *It* is the phone call from the doctor's office recommending you come back for a few more tests. *It* is the boss or the coworker or the schedule that makes working seem more like dying every day. *It* is the problem that you just can't seem to solve no matter what you do.

No matter what *it* is that you are facing, *it* won't have the last word when you pray it through. This is because prayer marches the problem into the presence of the One who can solve it. Prayer faces *it* by facing God immediately, consistently, doggedly, and hopefully. Prayer confesses, "I can't handle it, but God can. And since he can, I have hope!"

How do we pray that kind of prayer? By being persistent, like Elijah. Remember how he approached the throne of God when the widow's son passed away?

"Elijah cried out to the LORD, 'O LORD my God, why have you brought tragedy to this widow who has opened her home to me, causing her son to die?' And he stretched himself out over the child three times and cried out to the LORD, 'O LORD my God, please let this child's life return to him.' The LORD heard Elijah's prayer, and the life of the child returned, and he revived!" (1 Kings 17:20–22 NLT).

Three times he pressed his body against the boy's, begging for life to return. The first time did nothing. The second time did nothing. The third time brought the miracle. Importantly, Elijah had no precedent for such a request. At this point in biblical history, no person had ever been reclaimed from the grave. All Elijah had to go on was his faith in his *living* God. And that faith kept him praying even when others would have lost hope.

Let that be the rallying cry for your prayer life each and every day. Don't give up. Keep bringing *it* before the Father, who loves you and can do all things. Pray it through.

1. Think about what *it* represents right now—that primary concern troubling you, wringing you out, and dragging you down. How is *it* affecting your life right now?

[17] Some time later the son of the woman who owned the house became ill. He grew worse and worse, and finally stopped breathing. [18] She said to Elijah, "What do you have against me, man of God? Did you come to remind me of my sin and kill my son?"

[19] "Give me your son," Elijah replied. He took him from her arms, carried him to the upper room where he was staying, and laid him on his bed. [20] Then he cried out to the LORD, "LORD my God, have you brought tragedy even on this widow I am staying with, by causing her son to die?" [21] Then he stretched himself out on the boy three times and cried out to the LORD, "LORD my God, let this boy's life return to him!"

1 KINGS 17:17–21

2. In the ancient world, people often interpreted tragedy through the lens of divine punishment. How does this explain the widow's comment in verse 18? In what ways have you seen this same attitude among people today?

Note what Elijah didn't do. He didn't react to the widow's reaction. He didn't question her behavior. He understood that she was hurting and gave her grace. Grace was his gift to the mother. Prayer was his strategy for the tragedy. . . .

Elijah was silent before the mother, but he was resistless before God. "He stretched himself out on the child." He extended his adult body over the lifeless form. "Let this child's soul come back to him" (1 Kings 17:21 NKJV).

He didn't learn to pray like this in Prophet Training 101. He did this because he believed "the LORD God of Israel lives" (verse 1 NKJV). Elijah believed in a *living* God. Everywhere else, death. The land was dead from the famine. Livestock were dead from the drought. Crops were dead from thirst. The hope of the mother was dead. The boy was dead. But *Yahweh* was alive! Since God was, in Elijah's book, alive, and since the boy was, in Elijah's bed, dead, he took the case of the latter to the former.[10]

3. Elijah was silent before the mother but relentless in God's presence. What did Elijah understand about the God he served when it came to dealing with this tragedy? What did he comprehend about the importance of persistence in his prayers?

4. Elijah's story encourages you to pray persistently, even when the situation seems overwhelming. What are some of the longest requests you've been bringing to God? What requests or crises have you allowed to drop out of your prayers?

[1] Then Jesus told his disciples a parable to show them that they should al-
ways pray and not give up. [2] He said: "In a certain town there was a judge
who neither feared God nor cared what people thought. [3] And there was a
widow in that town who kept coming to him with the plea, 'Grant me justice
against my adversary.'
[4] "For some time he refused. But finally he said to himself, 'Even though
I don't fear God or care what people think, [5] yet because this widow keeps
bothering me, I will see that she gets justice, so that she won't eventually
come and attack me!'"
[6] And the Lord said, "Listen to what the unjust judge says. [7] And will not God
bring about justice for his chosen ones, who cry out to him day and night?
Will he keep putting them off? [8] I tell you, he will see that they get justice, and
quickly. However, when the Son of Man comes, will he find faith on the earth?"

LUKE 18:1-8

5. Parables in the ancient world typically communicated one primary point. What would you say is the primary point of this parable that Jesus told to his disciples?

6. Jesus wanted his followers to "pray and not give up" (verse 1). Where are you most in danger of losing heart right now? What will you do to persist instead?

STUDY 3

PRAY WITH CONFIDENCE

You've probably noticed the author of 1 Kings moves the descriptions of Elijah's life along fairly efficiently. The text moves quickly from a throne room to a wilderness to a Gentile town named Zarephath. Descriptions are sparse. Adjectives are few and far between.

So let's pause and really put ourselves in Elijah's shoes. He arrived in Zarephath after a hundred-mile march, as thirsty as he was dusty. He found a widow with almost no provisions, but he encouraged her to have faith. In true prophetic form, he declared, "This is what the LORD, the God of Israel, says: 'The jar of flour will not be used up and the jug of oil will not run dry until the day the LORD sends rain on the land'" (1 Kings 17:14).

And it came true! The flour kept flowing. The oil never ran out. The needs of Elijah, the widow, and her son were met day after day. We don't know how long Elijah stayed in this home, but the drought itself lasted more than three years. So we can be sure a familiarity developed between the prophet and the family.

Elijah and the widow must have felt as if their troubles were at an end. They had food, water, and shelter. What could go wrong?

The context helps us understand Elijah's mindset when he heard that the widow's son had died. According to the story, the son became ill, then grew worse, and then stopped breathing. This was a gradual illness that Elijah and the widow would have witnessed.

Notice how Elijah brought the matter to God's attention when the young man finally breathed his last: "Then he cried out to the LORD and said, 'O LORD my God, have You also brought tragedy on the widow with whom I lodge, by killing her son?'" (verse 20 NKJV).

Whoa! We might feel like the prophet was getting a little ahead of his skis. How dare anyone talk to God that way? Especially someone who was supposed to be a holy man!

But that's missing the point. Elijah was shocked by the sudden death of this boy he had helped nourish. He had heard the widow's anger, and he likely felt that same emotion himself. After all, he had asked her to trust him—to trust his God in spite of her fear. Had they come through so much only to crash and burn at the end?

Elijah didn't stuff this emotion down or pretend he didn't feel it. No, he marched to God's throne with familiarity, confidence, and boldness. He carried his emotions to God and poured them out in prayer. And, the text says, "The LORD heard Elijah's cry" (verse 22).

1. David wrote, "Trust in [God] at all times, you people; pour out your hearts to him" (Psalm 62:8). Most of us recognize that emotions are part of life, but many of us behave as if they shouldn't be part of our faith—that we shouldn't "pour out our hearts" to God. Look again at 1 Kings 17:8–24. What emotions are present in those verses?

2. Now read Psalm 22:1–11. What kind of emotions is David comfortable expressing to God? What does David profess to know about God even as he makes his complaints?

3. In the scales below, mark an *X* through the number of how comfortable you feel expressing the following emotions to *God*. Then circle the number for how comfortable you feel expressing these same emotions to other *people*.

Anger

1	2	3	4	5	6	7	8	9	10
[uncomfortable]									[comfortable]

Fear

1	2	3	4	5	6	7	8	9	10
[uncomfortable]									[comfortable]

Doubt

1	2	3	4	5	6	7	8	9	10
[uncomfortable]									[comfortable]

Annoyance or irritation

1	2	3	4	5	6	7	8	9	10
[uncomfortable]									[comfortable]

What stands out when you consider your responses? If you see a gap between your marks, why might you be viewing God one way and people another way?

Elijah prayed passionately. Dramatically. Emotionally. Thunderously. Begging. Pleading.

For many people, this is a new concept of prayer. We think of speaking softly before God or "talking to the man upstairs." But agonizing before God? Storming heaven with prayers? Pounding on the door of the Most High? Wrestling on our knees with God? Isn't such prayer irreverent? Isn't such prayer presumptuous?

It would be had God not invited us to pray as such. We do not swagger into God's presence, but neither do we cower. We are not bossy in our prayers, but neither are we mousy in our requests. We take courage and step confidently into the front door of the throne room of God, having been invited by him and escorted in by his Son. We embrace God as Father, kneel before him as Lord, and earnestly make our requests known, not because of what we have achieved, but because of what Christ has done. Jesus spilled his blood for us. We can pour out our hearts before God.

The irreverent one, then, is not the one who dares to make bold requests. The irreverent one is the one who mumbles feeble appeals for favors and perks.[11]

4. Paul wrote, "The Spirit you received does not make you slaves . . . rather, the Spirit you received brought about your adoption to sonship" (Romans 8:15). If you are a child of God, you have been invited into his presence. When you come before God, do you picture him more as a distant monarch or a loving parent? What might change in the way you prayed if you pictured him more as a heavenly *father*?

5. Paul also wrote, "Now if we are children, then we are heirs—heirs of God and co-heirs with Christ" (Romans 8:17). Jesus earned the right for you to appear before the Creator of the universe. How should that reality influence the way you pray?

> 14 Therefore, since we have a great high priest who has ascended into heaven,
> Jesus the Son of God, let us hold firmly to the faith we profess. 15 For we do
> not have a high priest who is unable to empathize with our weaknesses, but
> we have one who has been tempted in every way, just as we are—yet he did
> not sin. 16 Let us then approach God's throne of grace with confidence, so that
> we may receive mercy and find grace to help us in our time of need.
>
> HEBREWS 4:14-16

6. God actually *invites* you to pray with boldness. You can approach his throne of grace with confidence. What is one bold request that you need to make to God today?

Heavenly Father, I make this bold request of you today . . .

CATCH UP AND READ AHEAD

Connect with a fellow group member this week and discuss some of the key insights from this session. Use any of the following prompts to help guide your discussion.

- What ideas or concepts felt confusing from the study material in this session? What questions would you like to have answered?
- When you look back on your life, what are some of the ways that God has proven himself to be faithful and trustworthy?
- How would you like to grow when it comes to being persistent in your prayers? How would you like God to encourage you in this regard?
- How did the content you covered in this session encourage you to express your honest emotions to God?
- What does it mean to be *confident* in approaching the Lord while also being *humble* before him? How do you achieve this balance in your prayers?

Use this time to go back and complete any of the study and reflection questions from previous days that you weren't able to finish. Make a note below of any revelations you've had and reflect on any growth or personal insights you've gained.

Read chapters 5–6 in *Unbreakable Courage* before the next group gathering. Use the space below to note anything in those chapters that stands out to you or encourages you.

WEEK 3 *at a Glance*

THIS WEEK'S READING	Chapters 5–6 in *Unbreakable Courage*
GROUP MEETING	Read the Welcome and Connect with the group (page 49) Watch the video and take notes (pages 50–51) Discuss the questions that follow (page 52) Respond to the teaching and Close (pages 53–54)
PERSONAL STUDIES: Study 1 Study 2 Study 3	 "A History of Rebellion" (pages 56–59) "Playing Both Sides" (pages 60–63) "A Picture of Justice" (pages 64–66)
CATCH UP AND READ AHEAD (BEFORE WEEK 4 MEETING)	Connect with someone in your group Complete any unfinished personal studies (page 67)
NEXT WEEK'S READING	Chapters 7–8 in *Unbreakable Courage*

SESSION THREE

BEHIND ENEMY LINES

Then Elijah said to them, "I am the only one of the Lord*'s prophets left, but Baal has four hundred and fifty prophets. Get two bulls for us. Let Baal's prophets choose one for themselves, and let them cut it into pieces and put it on the wood but not set fire to it. I will prepare the other bull and put it on the wood but not set fire to it. Then you call on the name of your god, and I will call on the name of the* Lord*. The god who answers by fire—he is God."*

1 KINGS 18:22-24

Elijah confronts Ahab and flees to the Kerith Ravine
(1 Kings 17:1–6)

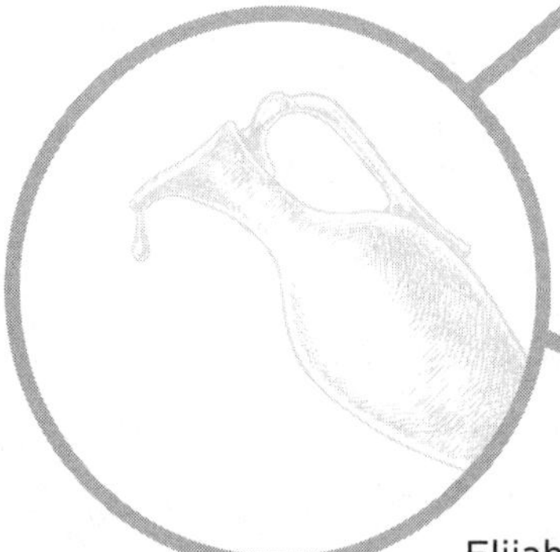

Elijah goes to the widow's home at Zarephath
(1 Kings 17:7–24)

Elijah confronts the false prophets at Mount Carmel
(1 Kings 18:16–40)

WELCOME | READ ON YOUR OWN

To confront or not to confront. That is the question. You've been in situations where a confrontation seemed possible. You may have encountered such a situation recently. Someone treated you rudely, for example. Or, worse, they disrespected somebody you care about. Maybe you found yourself involved in a clash of values with a coworker, or a neighbor, or a guy standing in line behind you at the store. Maybe there was a protest in the street or a rally promoting a way of thinking you know to be harmful.

Whatever the situation might be, there comes a moment when you must make a decision. *Do I say something? Should I step up and do something? Will I stand up for what I know to be right even if it risks causing a scene?*

It's safe to say that modern Christians typically avoid public confrontation whenever possible. We want to be nice. We want to be loving and compassionate. So we stuff down our irritation and indignation. Oftentimes, this is the right call. After all, it was Jesus himself who reminded us to go the extra mile and turn the other cheek.

And yet.

Sometimes we can't stuff it down. We can't let it go. We find ourselves in situations where apathy is worse than confrontation—a situation where taking a stand is not only the courageous thing to do but the responsible way to behave as citizens of a heavenly kingdom. We still act in ways that are appropriate for citizens of heaven . . . *but we do act.*

Elijah found himself in that kind of situation. He needed to take a stand. It was imperative for him to take action. And in doing so, he initiated one of the most impressive and inspiring confrontations recorded in the Bible. Let's look at that moment together.

CONNECT | 10 MINUTES

Get this session started by discussing one of these questions:

- What wars or conflicts are center stage in the news today? What in particular is driving those conflicts?

— *or* —

- When have you felt harassed or exposed because you were different from those around you? What did you do in response?

WATCH | 25 MINUTES

Now watch the video for this session. Below is an outline of the key points covered during the teaching. Record any key concepts that stand out to you.

OUTLINE

I. Elijah understood what it is like to live behind enemy lines.

A. Most of the inhabitants of Israel no longer served the God of Abraham, Isaac, and Jacob.

B. Led by Ahab and Jezebel, Israel had turned to worshiping the false gods of the Canaanites.

C. This idolatry had Satan's fingerprints all over it—rebellion against God.

D. Israel was now especially hostile to prophets from God like Elijah.

II. God sent Elijah into enemy territory because the situation was intolerable to him.

A. God did not want the depravity of pagan worship for his people.

B. So after three years of drought, he instructed Elijah to present himself to Ahab.

C. At this time, Ahab and Jezebel were still actively seeking to kill Elijah.

D. It took unbreakable courage for Elijah to present himself to his enemies.

III. Elijah called for a contest between God and the false Canaanite gods.

A. This was the Lord revealing just how powerless Satan was before him.

B. The false prophets spent hours calling on their false gods—but with no result.

C. Elijah called for twelve buckets of water to be poured over his offering.

D. God likes to show up and show off in a way that leaves no doubt who is in charge!

IV. What this story teaches about how to be strong and courageous in a fallen world.

A. Heaven opened and fire fell, consuming the water, rocks, wood, and even the dust.

B. For the first time in three generations, the people of Israel cried out, "The Lord—he is God!"

C. This world is enemy territory, but the God we serve is stronger than the devil.

D. God has sent you on a mission behind enemy lines—so step out with your comrades-in-arms.

NOTES

DISCUSS | 35 MINUTES

Discuss what you just watched by answering the following questions.

1. To say that our world is "enemy territory" is to recognize Satan's influence across the globe—not to mention across human history. In your own words, how would you describe who Satan is and what he desires to do in our world?

2. Ask one or two volunteers to read aloud 1 Kings 18:25–40, which describes the confrontation between Elijah and the false prophets. What do those verses teach about the values and the worldview of those who worshiped Baal and Asherah?

3. Where do you see similar values or a similar worldview on display in our culture?

4. Read aloud John 3:16–18. God sent Elijah behind enemy lines because he wanted to rescue his people from depravity. How does Elijah's mission compare with that of Jesus? In what ways was Jesus sent behind enemy lines to rescue us from depravity?

5. Confrontations such as those we read about between God's prophets and false prophets might seem like a thing of the past, but it is also necessary for modern believers to demonstrate real courage as we live behind enemy lines. When have you recently had an opportunity to take a stand for your faith? What happened as a result?

RESPOND | 10 MINUTES

When it comes to choosing conflict for righteous reasons, there is no greater example than Christ himself. The Gospels of Matthew, Mark, and Luke relate one moment in particular that came near the end of Jesus' public ministry. In fact, it occurred the last week before his crucifixion. Jesus rode into Jerusalem on a foal of a donkey and heard the crowds sing out, "Hosanna! Blessed is he who comes in the name of the Lord!" (Mark 11:9). He then stepped into the temple courts. Here is what Matthew records happened next:

> 12 Jesus entered the temple courts and drove out all who were buying and selling there. He overturned the tables of the money changers and the benches of those selling doves. 13 "It is written," he said to them, "'My house will be called a house of prayer,' but you are making it 'a den of robbers.'" 14 The blind and the lame came to him at the temple, and he healed them. 15 But when the chief priests and the teachers of the law saw the wonderful things he did and the children shouting in the temple courts, "Hosanna to the Son of David," they were indignant.
>
> MATTHEW 21:12-15

Jesus denounced the moneychangers and merchants for transforming the temple into a "den of robbers." His anger was ignited by the injustice taking place within its walls. Based on what you know of God's character, why would this have been so egregious to him?

There are times when Christians should respond to the world with grace and other times when they must take a stand for the values of God's kingdom. What have you learned that helps you discern when conflict or confrontation is necessary?

CLOSE | 10 MINUTES

Conclude this session by acknowledging that you and everyone in your group are living behind enemy lines. You are working, serving, and raising your families in enemy-occupied territory. Ask God to strengthen you and bless you with discernment each day. Specifically, ask that you would have clarity when it comes to your mission for God's kingdom and that you would know when the time has come to take a firm stand for the values of that kingdom. Use the space below to write down any requests so you and your group members can pray about them in the week ahead.

Name	Request

SESSION THREE

PERSONAL STUDY

You are like a paratrooper in God's army. You are a member of an elite force that has been tasked with the mission of parachuting behind enemy lines. Your presence creates chaos and confusion in the enemy's ranks. For this reason, the more you press forward, the more your enemy will attempt to push you back. As the apostle John wrote, "The whole world is under the control of the evil one" (1 John 5:19), and he wants to maintain the existing state of affairs. God, on the other hand, wants to upset this status quo. The Bible tells us that "God so loved the world that he gave his one and only Son" (John 3:16)—for the people who have fallen prey to the enemy. In this personal study, you will take a closer look at how the enemy operates and the mission God has for you to undo his plans. Continue writing down your responses to share with the group, and if you are reading *Unbreakable Courage* alongside this study, first review chapters 5–6 of the book.

STUDY 1

A HISTORY OF REBELLION

The rebels are usually the good guys. At least, that's how it is portrayed in movies. In our modern entertainment, groups that rebel against a larger force are almost always portrayed as protagonists. Think *Star Wars*. Or *Braveheart*. Or *Avatar*. Or any other story where squads of scrappy insurgents take down a bloated, uncaring, overpowered empire.

We like those kinds of stories. Maybe it's because we like to root for the little guy. Or maybe it's because we don't like what we see today with corporations or governments. Or maybe . . . just maybe . . . it's because we have a bit of rebel in us as well.

The story of the Bible is the story of God's love and purpose for his children. He created us and desired for us to be a part of his heavenly family. From the beginning, God wanted us to be part of his perfect world—a garden of Eden existence. The whole earth would be Eden-ish. God would make our world a garden full of family.

Then came the rebellion. It started with Satan, who in his heart rejected God's authority and attempted to ascend above the Almighty. When his rebellion failed, he and his angelic followers were cast out of heaven (see Revelation 12:7–9), and he then came across Adam and Eve. You know *that* story. Satan caused Adam and Eve to doubt God's good intentions toward them. He tempted them to disobey the Lord . . . and they took the bait.

In this way, the enemy's rebellion extended to humanity. Sin entered the world. We've all been victims of the darkness and chaos ever since.

This is the backdrop to Elijah's story. God didn't walk away after humanity's attempted rebellion. He didn't give up on humans. Instead, he worked behind the scenes to provide a plan of redemption through which all might be saved. Part of that plan involved re-revealing himself to the world through a small group we call the Jewish people. God gave them his laws and his presence and his promise. All they had to do was obey.

By the time Elijah burst onto the scene, some five hundred years had passed since Joshua led the conquest of the promised land. These years had seen not only the nation of Israel break into two kingdoms but also its people drift far away from God. The kingdom of Israel in particular had become a nation of idolaters.

A nation of rebels once more.

1. Rebellion is fundamentally a reaction against authority. If you are being completely honest, to what degree do you typically rebel against (or feel a desire to push back against) authority figures in the following areas of your life?

Authority figures at work

1 2 3 4 5 6 7 8 9 10
[not much] [quite a lot]

Authority figures at home

1 2 3 4 5 6 7 8 9 10
[not much] [quite a lot]

Authority figures in government

1 2 3 4 5 6 7 8 9 10
[not much] [quite a lot]

Authority figures within the church

1 2 3 4 5 6 7 8 9 10
[not much] [quite a lot]

2. If we say that sin is rebellion against God, it means God has a right to exert his authority not only in our world but also in our lives. How would you summarize the source of that authority? (In other words, why does God have authority in your life?)

> 22 "Should you not fear me?" declares the LORD.
> "Should you not tremble in my presence?
> I made the sand a boundary for the sea,
> an everlasting barrier it cannot cross.
> The waves may roll, but they cannot prevail;
> they may roar, but they cannot cross it.
> 23 But these people have stubborn and rebellious hearts;
> they have turned aside and gone away.
> 24 They do not say to themselves,
> 'Let us fear the LORD our God,
> who gives autumn and spring rains in season,
> who assures us of the regular weeks of harvest.'
> 25 Your wrongdoings have kept these away;
> your sins have deprived you of good."
>
> JEREMIAH 5:22-25

3. Jeremiah was a prophet who ministered in the southern kingdom of Judah some 250 years after Elijah. One of the reasons the Israelite people—both those in the northern and southern kingdoms—had rebelled against God was because they did not fear him. In your own words, what does it mean to fear the Lord?

4. God pointed out that the people's wrongdoing had "kept" his blessings away and "deprived" them of the good he wanted to do for them (verse 25). Think back to a season when your lifestyle was out of alignment with God's values and priorities—a season when you rebelled against God by your choices. What were you attempting to gain by making those choices? What were the results of those choices in your life?

The name *Satan* is not mentioned in the Elijah narrative, but his greasy fingerprints are on every page. This is more than Elijah versus Ahab and Jezebel. This is God versus Satan. . . .

Ever since Satan was cast out of heaven, he's been trying to populate hell with God's children. He especially directed his attacks on Israel, God's chosen nation. God's promised plan was to bring a Redeemer to the world through the bloodline of Abraham, the father of the Jews. By destroying the Jews, Satan hoped to derail God's plan.

By the time Elijah appears on the scene, God's plan seems in jeopardy. Where are God's people? Where are God's prophets? The nation has turned from the living God to the lying messages of Baal and Asherah.[12]

5. Paul wrote that your struggle in this world "is not against flesh and blood" but against "the powers of this dark world" (Ephesians 6:12). How often do you consider that you have a *real* enemy who is seeking to thwart God's plans for your life? Why is it critical not to forget that you are living on a battlefield between good and evil?

6. Like Elijah, you live in a society that stands in opposition to God's will and purposes. Also like Elijah, however, you can be sure that God hasn't given up on our world. Where do you see hope for revival in your community? In your nation as a whole?

STUDY 2

PLAYING BOTH SIDES

Let's get ready to rumble! This was a famous catchphrase first used to introduce professional wrestling matches back in the mid-1980s. Of course, there was no professional wrestling in Elijah's day. It's unlikely there were any ringside announcers or commentators present at Mount Carmel when Elijah squared off against hundreds of false prophets.

Even so, the event had the spectacle-like feel of a professional wrestling event. Elijah, as you will recall, had announced a drought in Israel. In doing so, he proclaimed Baal—the supposed god of rain and the fertile land it brought—to be powerless. A long journey for Elijah followed, with God first sending him to the Kerith Ravine and then to Zarephath. In time, the Lord moved Elijah on again, sending him back to the court of King Ahab.

When the king saw him, he said, "Is that you, you troubler of Israel?" (1 Kings 18:17). Elijah—bold as ever—replied, "I have not made trouble for Israel . . . but you and your father's family have" (verse 18). Elijah then went on to issue a direct challenge: "Now summon the people from all over Israel to meet me on Mount Carmel. And bring the four hundred and fifty prophets of Baal and the four hundred prophets of Asherah" (verse 19).

Let's get ready to rumble! The match was set. The players arrived on the designated day. Interestingly, there is no record of Elijah addressing Ahab once he entered the arena. Nor did he speak to the false prophets who were his opponents. Instead, he addressed the people of Israel and Judah. He spoke to them directly—even sternly.

"Elijah went before the people and said, 'How long will you waver between two opinions? If the Lord is God, follow him; but if Baal is God, follow him.' But the people said nothing" (verse 21). This was a critical moment. Elijah was about to demonstrate the superiority of God over the false deities. But in that moment, the people of Israel were trying to straddle the fence in terms of their worship. They didn't want to turn their backs on the God of their forefathers. But they also weren't willing to let go of Baal and Asherah.

Today we call this "playing both sides," but it boils down to a single word: *hypocrisy*. The Israelites of Elijah's day were hypocrites. They pretended to believe one thing but practiced something different. They imitated intimacy with God in public but in private embraced idolatry. This dual way of life was deadly for the children of Israel. And it's deadly for us today.

1. As a concept, hypocrisy can be difficult to pin down. It's something we all struggle with to different degrees, but it's often easier to spot in others than in ourselves.

How would you define or describe what it means to be hypocritical?

What are some examples of hypocrisy you have seen recently in the news?

What are some recent examples of hypocrisy you have personally witnessed?

2. The Israelites identified themselves as God's chosen people, but the nations around them worshiped idols as a way of attempting to secure more food, more children, more safety from enemies, and so on. Where do you typically feel pressure to combine or assimilate your worship of God with the systems or worldviews of our culture?

> 14 "Now fear the LORD and serve him with all faithfulness. Throw away the gods your ancestors worshiped beyond the Euphrates River and in Egypt, and serve the LORD. 15 But if serving the LORD seems undesirable to you, then choose for yourselves this day whom you will serve, whether the gods your ancestors served beyond the Euphrates, or the gods of the Amorites, in whose land you are living. But as for me and my household, we will serve the LORD."
>
> 16 Then the people answered, "Far be it from us to forsake the LORD to serve other gods! 17 It was the LORD our God himself who brought us and our parents up out of Egypt, from that land of slavery, and performed those great signs before our eyes. He protected us on our entire journey and among all the nations through which we traveled. 18 And the LORD drove out before us all the nations, including the Amorites, who lived in the land. We too will serve the LORD, because he is our God."
>
> JOSHUA 24:14–18

3. This dialogue between Joshua and the Israelites occurred at the end of the conquest of the promised land. What did Joshua see would be the problem if the people did not separate themselves from the Canaanites? What choice was he putting before them?

4. Notice how the people responded. They recalled how the Lord God had brought them out of Egypt, protected them, and drove out nations before them. What type of "memory loss" had happened to the people by Elijah's day? What type of "memory loss" happens to Christians today when it comes to recalling God's act of faithfulness?

Elijah looked out over his compatriots and asked a Continental Divide-level question: "How long are you going to struggle with the two choices?" (1 Kings 18:21 NASB). The literal wording in Hebrew is "How long will you keep hopping between two crevices?" The question conjures up an image of a person dancing between two cracks in a rock. It's an idiomatic expression that equals "How long will you try to have it both ways?"

The people were dancing in their devotion. They were wavering in their allegiance, "hobbling back and forth" (CEB) in their commitment, "limping" (ESV) along in their faith, "halting" (KJV) in their dedication. Hopscotch commitment. In and out. Their religion was half God, half Baal. They changed uniforms depending on the latest fashion.

Would you be willing to ask God to reveal any areas in your life where you are doing the same? We cannot win both the applause of people and the "well done" of Christ. What is your choice? Is your loyalty shifting back and forth depending on the trend of the day or the opinions of your peers? Do *you* play both sides?[13]

5. Take a moment to answer the questions from the quotation above. Where are you attempting to play both sides when it comes to serving Christ or serving yourself?

6. As mentioned previously, it is often much easier to spot hypocrisy in others than to catch its growth in your own life. What are some steps you can take (or systems you can put in place) to identify hypocrisy in your own beliefs, thoughts, and actions?

STUDY 3

A PICTURE OF JUSTICE

Let's admit it. The confrontation between Elijah and the prophets of Baal at Mount Carmel is interesting reading. The imagery alone is fantastic.

The false prophets are dancing and prancing, jumping and shouting, flailing and flapping in their efforts to catch the attention of something with no eyes, ears, heart, or mind. The scene has its humorous moments, with Elijah providing commentary worthy of the peanut gallery: "Shout louder! . . . Perhaps he is deep in thought, or busy, or traveling. Maybe he is sleeping and must be awakened" (1 Kings 18:27).

This same prophet, confident and strong, then rebuilds the altar to the Lord, which had been torn down, stone by stone. We can picture the assurance in his face as he instructs the young men to pour buckets of water over the sacrifice. "Again," he says. "And again." Of course, the most powerful visual of all is the fire streaking down from the sky to consume the bull, evaporate the water, and char the stone. Mission accomplished.

But the story doesn't end with that fiery declaration of God's dominance. There is a coda—one that makes readers uncomfortable: "Then Elijah commanded them, 'Seize the prophets of Baal. Don't let anyone get away!' They seized them, and Elijah had them brought down to the Kishon Valley and slaughtered there" (verse 40).

None of us can read that text without a wince. It doesn't sit well in our modern mindset to see a man of God brandishing a sword and executing several hundred men. But remember, those false prophets weren't just men. According to scholars, "At times of crisis, Baal's followers sacrificed their children, apparently the firstborn of the community, to gain personal prosperity. The Bible called this practice 'detestable.' "[14]

Under their leadership, the people of God had abandoned their calling. God did not want such wickedness to continue. So he intervened. Through the sword of Elijah, the Lord of heaven let justice roll down like waters.

This is something we need to keep in mind as we live and minister behind enemy lines—that justice will be done. Today, it may seem as though the wicked prosper and the righteous falter, but that will not be the case forever. Indeed, that will not be the case much longer in the broad scope of history.

Our King will return, and in justice he will reclaim his territory.

1. What are your immediate reactions when you read about Elijah ordering the slaughter of the prophets of Baal? What questions does this raise up in you?

2. One definition of *justice* is "the maintenance of what is just or right by the exercise of authority or power and the assignment of deserved reward or punishment."[15] In its simplest form, justice means to set things right—and it is important to the Lord. What instructions does God give to his followers about justice in these verses?

Passage	Instructions God Gives to His Followers
Psalm 82:2–3	
Isaiah 1:17	
Micah 6:8	
Luke 11:42	

3. Read Deuteronomy 13:1–5. Elijah called for the execution of the false prophets after their god failed to produce fire from heaven. What was Elijah's basis for taking this action under the law of God? When you consider the damage that idolatry did throughout the history of God's people, why might the Lord have established this law?

> 9 What shall we conclude then? Do we have any advantage? Not at all! For we have already made the charge that Jews and Gentiles alike are all under the power of sin. . . . 22 There is no difference between Jew and Gentile, 23 for all have sinned and fall short of the glory of God, 24 and all are justified freely by his grace through the redemption that came by Christ Jesus. 25 God presented Christ as a sacrifice of atonement, through the shedding of his blood—to be received by faith. He did this to demonstrate his righteousness, because in his forbearance he had left the sins committed beforehand unpunished— 26 he did it to demonstrate his righteousness at the present time, so as to be just and the one who justifies those who have faith in Jesus.
>
> ROMANS 3:9, 22-26

4. Pastor Tim Keller wrote, "Biblical justice is not first of all a set of bullet points or a set of rules and guidelines. It is rooted in the very character of God and it is the out-working of that character, which is never less than just."[16] What does Paul say that every person is guilty of doing—regardless of whether they are a Jew or Gentile?

5. We all are deserving of God's justice and judgment because we "all have sinned" (verse 23). But what did God choose to do instead? What does it mean that God offered Christ "as a sacrifice of atonement" (verse 25) for the justice we deserved?

6. Read Revelation 19:17–21. Satan is your true enemy, and one day his rule will come to an end. What hope does this give you when you look at the state of the world today? How does it comfort you to know that God *will* exact his justice against evil?

CATCH UP AND READ AHEAD

Connect with a fellow group member this week and discuss some of the key insights from this session. Use any of the following prompts to help guide your discussion.

- What struck you as most interesting or surprising from this session? What parts of this session were the most challenging for you?
- Rebellion, at its core, is a reaction against authority. How does that play out in our lives when it comes to God's authority over us?
- It's easier to spot hypocrisy in others than in ourselves. What steps will you take to identify hypocrisy in your beliefs, thoughts, and actions?
- One day, God will pour out his wrath against sin, Satan, and all wickedness. What emotions do you experience when you think about that future day?
- How can you, as citizens of God's kingdom, help each other minister and thrive even though you live behind enemy lines?

Use this time to go back and complete any of the study and reflection questions from previous days that you weren't able to finish. Make a note below of any revelations you've had and reflect on any growth or personal insights you've gained.

Read chapters 7–8 in *Unbreakable Courage* before the next group gathering. Use the space below to note anything in those chapters that stands out to you or encourages you.

WEEK 4 *at a Glance*

THIS WEEK'S READING	Chapters 7–8 in *Unbreakable Courage*
GROUP MEETING	Read the Welcome and Connect with the group (page 71) Watch the video and take notes (pages 72–73) Discuss the questions that follow (page 74) Respond to the teaching and Close (pages 75–76)
PERSONAL STUDIES: Study 1 Study 2 Study 3	 "God Knows Best" (pages 78–81) "God Understands" (pages 82–85) "God Speaks" (pages 86–90)
CATCH UP AND READ AHEAD (BEFORE WEEK 5 MEETING)	Connect with someone in your group Complete any unfinished personal studies (page 91)
NEXT WEEK'S READING	Chapters 9–10 in *Unbreakable Courage*

SESSION FOUR

A STORM ON THE HORIZON

Now Ahab told Jezebel everything Elijah had done and how he had killed all the prophets with the sword. So Jezebel sent a messenger to Elijah to say, "May the gods deal with me, be it ever so severely, if by this time tomorrow I do not make your life like that of one of them." Elijah was afraid and ran for his life. When he came to Beersheba in Judah, he left his servant there, while he himself went a day's journey into the wilderness. He came to a broom bush, sat down under it and prayed that he might die. "I have had enough, Lord," he said. "Take my life; I am no better than my ancestors."

1 KINGS 19:1–4

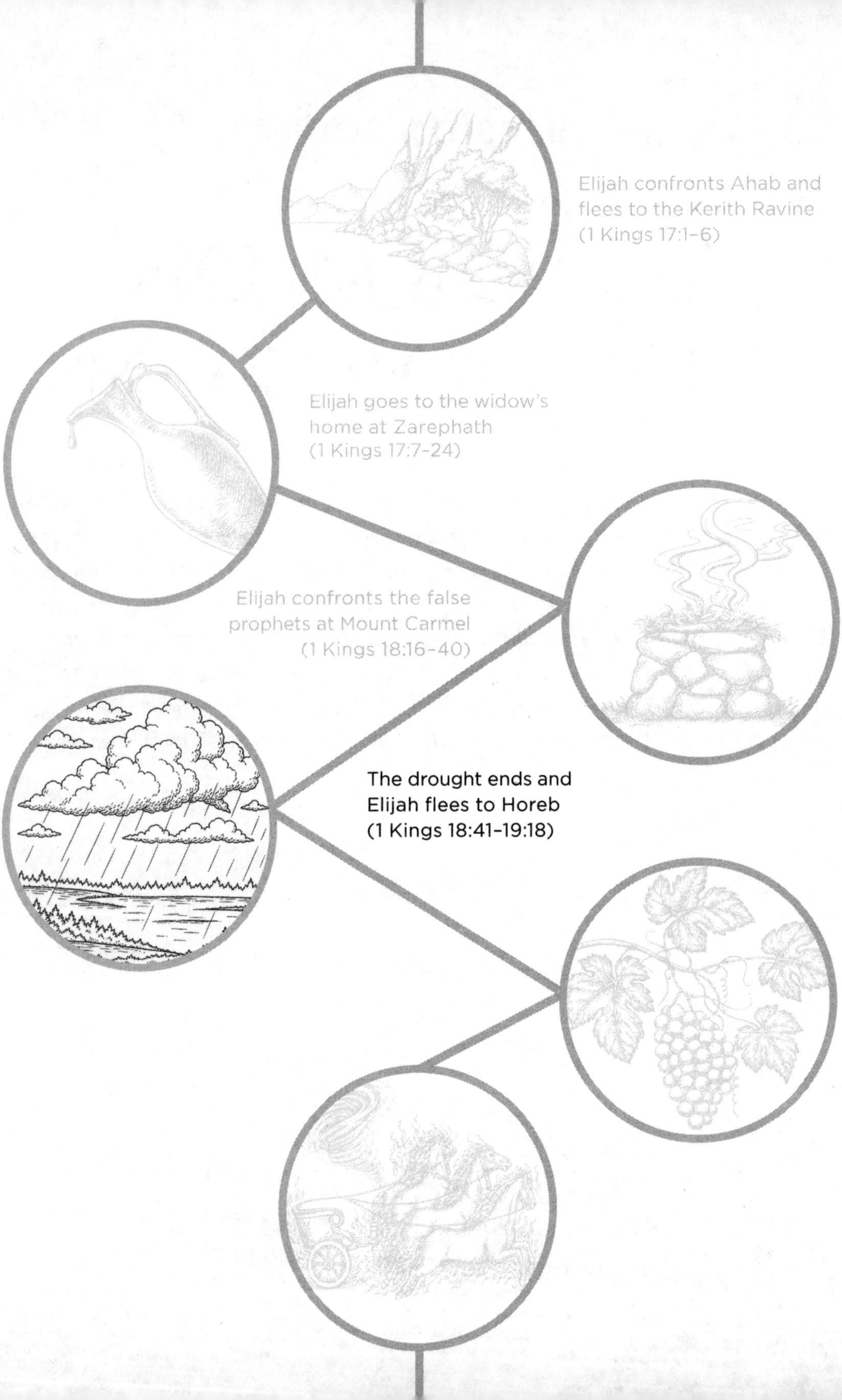
Elijah confronts Ahab and flees to the Kerith Ravine (1 Kings 17:1–6)
Elijah goes to the widow's home at Zarephath (1 Kings 17:7–24)
Elijah confronts the false prophets at Mount Carmel (1 Kings 18:16–40)
The drought ends and Elijah flees to Horeb (1 Kings 18:41–19:18)

WELCOME | READ ON YOUR OWN

If there's anyone who had a good reason to be scared of storms, it was Roy Sullivan. The National Weather Service reports that the chance of a person being struck by lightning is 1 in 15,300.[17] Roy, a park ranger in Virginia, significantly beat those odds. In fact, he holds the Guinness World Record for the most lightning strikes survived by a human being.

Roy's encounters started in 1942 when a strike streaked through his body and out through his big toe, causing him to lose the nail. He was hit again in 1969 and lost both eyebrows. A strike in 1970 left his shoulder seared, and another in 1972 set his hair on fire. Less than a year later, lightning seared his leg. Next came June of 1976, when a strike injured his ankle. The final strike occurred a year later, causing burns on his chest and stomach.[18]

Talk about a run of bad luck! (Or was it good luck that kept him alive?) Seven times Roy Sullivan received a zap from the clouds. Seven times he survived. Imagine how terrified he must have felt every time a storm cloud rolled in overhead.

The storm clouds were gathering as well in Elijah's story. In fact, he would be met by two different storms—and respond to them in two different ways.

The first storm was physical and a welcome sight after more than three years of drought. "The sky grew black with clouds, the wind rose, a heavy rain started falling" (1 Kings 18:45). The second storm was political and spiritual. It came from Jezebel, who told Elijah, "May the gods deal with me . . . if by this time tomorrow I do not make your life like that of one of the [false prophets]" (19:2).

We're going to explore both storms in this session—including Elijah's reaction to this threat in a way you would never expect. Even more, we're going to learn some powerful and practical tips for managing our own lives whenever we see a storm on the horizon.

CONNECT | 10 MINUTES

Get this session started by discussing one of these questions:

- What kind of weather event or natural disaster do you find most concerning for your community? Why?

— or —

- What is your go-to comfort food when you're feeling sad or disappointed?

WATCH | 25 MINUTES

Now watch the video for this session. Below is an outline of the key points covered during the teaching. Record any key concepts that stand out to you.

OUTLINE

I. The Lord told Elijah that the three-year drought in Israel was coming to an end.

A. The revival that broke out after the showdown on Mount Carmel led to an end to the drought.

B. God had set a time limit on how long his people's predicament would last.

C. Elijah told Ahab that he could hear "the sound of a heavy rain" (1 Kings 18:41).

D. Elijah's faith allowed him to view the Lord's promise as though it had already been fulfilled.

II. When the rain poured down, everyone in Israel rejoiced—except Queen Jezebel.

A. Jezebel made another threat against Elijah in what had been a series of threats.

B. We would expect Elijah to react with unbreakable courage . . . but instead he ran.

C. He ran more than a hundred miles away and collapsed under a broom bush.

D. Elijah despaired even of the strength to take another step.

III. What could cause our fearless hero to experience such a total collapse?

A. Elijah was physically exhausted. Everything that he had experienced (including a marathon-level run to get ahead of Ahab) had left him physically worn out.

B. Jezebel's threat was a morale buster. Elijah thought he had finally won after years of enduring her threats, but now she was after him even harder than before.

IV. God responded to Elijah with a critical prescription: nourishment and rest.

A. This episode reveals that seasons of sadness come to even the most steadfast and faithful of saints.

B. Refreshed by God, he traveled forty days and nights until he reached Horeb.

C. There God offered him encouragement and told him not everyone in Israel had bowed to Baal.

D. God will likewise refresh us, encourage us, and equip us to do the work we were made to do.

NOTES

DISCUSS | 35 MINUTES

Discuss what you just watched by answering the following questions.

1. God allowed the drought that devastated Israel to occur, but he also set a time limit on its duration. Both acts demonstrated his sovereignty. How would you explain the concept of God's sovereignty in your own words? What does it mean for us today?

2. Ask someone to read 1 Kings 18:41–46. Elijah had demonstrated incredible courage in the face of adversity and prevailed. He could have allowed the victory to go to his head. Instead, what does he do in this passage? What does this say about his character?

3. What else did Elijah do in this passage that reveals his steadfast faith? What does this story emphasize to you about the importance of persisting in prayer?

4. Now ask someone to read 1 Kings 19:1–10. What contrasts do you see between Elijah's actions here and those in the previous chapter? What are two reasons (presented in the teaching) as to why Elijah might have responded to Jezebel's message in this way?

5. When Elijah came to the end of his rope, God gave him a season of nourishment and rest. He also encouraged Elijah by telling him there were seven thousand people in Israel who had not "bowed down to Baal" (verse 18). When has the Lord given you a similar season of nourishment, rest, and encouragement? How did it change your outlook on the situation you were facing?

RESPOND | 10 MINUTES

We can be thankful that failure is a prominent theme in the Bible. Many of God's servants failed him and failed themselves on many occasions—just like we do.

Peter the disciple is a great example. This man, who typically acted before thinking, covered himself with shame on the night that Jesus was betrayed and arrested. After following the soldiers to the place where Jesus was interrogated before the high priest, three people accused Peter of being one of the Savior's disciples. Three times, Peter denied his Lord. It was a terrible failure that must have stuck with him like the smell of rotting fish.

Even so, Peter would not be defined by his failure:

> 15 When they had finished eating, Jesus said to Simon Peter, "Simon son of John, do you love me more than these?"
>
> "Yes, Lord," he said, "you know that I love you."
>
> Jesus said, "Feed my lambs."
>
> 16 Again Jesus said, "Simon son of John, do you love me?"
>
> He answered, "Yes, Lord, you know that I love you."
>
> Jesus said, "Take care of my sheep."
>
> 17 The third time he said to him, "Simon son of John, do you love me?" Peter was hurt because Jesus asked him the third time, "Do you love me?" He said, "Lord, you know all things; you know that I love you."
>
> Jesus said, "Feed my sheep."
>
> JOHN 21:15-17

What similarities do you see between the way that Jesus dealt with Peter's failure in this passage and the way that God dealt with Elijah's failure in 1 Kings 19:9–18?

Elijah's failure was in succumbing to fear and not trusting God. Peter's failure was in denying that he even knew Christ. We all fail God in different ways. When you recognize that you have failed, how should you respond? What are the appropriate next steps to take?

CLOSE | 10 MINUTES

Conclude this session by affirming the truth of God's sovereignty—that he is in charge no matter what storms or what struggles come your way. Ask God to provide for your needs of rest, nourishment, and encouragement this week. Ask also for the eyes and humility to recognize when you fail and for the wisdom to repent. Use the space below to write down any requests so you and your group members can pray about them in the week ahead.

Name	Request

SESSION FOUR

PERSONAL STUDY

C. S. Lewis wrote, "After each failure, ask forgiveness, pick yourself up, and try again. Very often what God first helps us towards is not the virtue itself but just this power of always trying again."[19] As you saw in this week's group time, God did not leave Elijah to just wallow in his failure. Instead, he met Elijah in the wilderness and divinely provided a loaf of baked bread and a jar of water for him. Later, at Mount Horeb, God revealed himself to Elijah and let him know that he was *not* the only person in Israel who still served the Lord. In this personal study, you will take a look at the events that led to this moment in Elijah's life, uncovering more important principles for how to maintain your faith even when you're filled with fear. Continue writing down your responses to share with the group, and if you are reading *Unbreakable Courage* alongside this study, first review chapters 7–8 of the book.

STUDY 1

GOD KNOWS BEST

One of the most wonderful things about kids is their capacity to trust.

Picture a five-year-old girl who has inched herself outward toward the edge of a playset. She's five feet off the ground, and her body knows it. She instinctively squats down and grabs one of the metal railings nearby to feel safe. But then her daddy steps forward. He smiles, holds out his arms, and says, "Jump!"

What will that little girl do? Jump. It may take a few seconds. It may take a little more prompting. But if she trusts her daddy, she will flex her knees and fly out over the edge at the sound of his voice. Can you see the joy on her face as he catches her and pulls her close to his chest? Can you see the way her daddy grins from ear to ear?

That's faith. It's trusting that another knows best, even when the situation or the circumstances seem murky in our eyes. Most five-year-olds understand that jumping from a playset is a bad idea—one that will bring painful consequences. But when Mommy or Daddy says "jump," they jump.

But do ten-year-olds have that same faith? What about fifteen-year-olds? What about fifty-five-year-olds? Sooner or later, we let go of faith in others and hold fast to faith in ourselves. *"I am the captain of my ship. I know what's best for me."*

As we have seen throughout this study, one of the wonderful (and incredible) things about Elijah is his unquestioning faith in his heavenly Father. When God said to confront the king and queen, Elijah thundered into their throne room with a declaration of drought. When God said a brook would satisfy his thirst and ravens retrieve his food, Elijah marched out into the wilderness with his knife and fork. When God said a widow would provide for his needs, Elijah encouraged her to bake a cake with her final bit of flour.

And when God said it was time for the rain to fall once more, Elijah spoke that promise to the king. He had faith in God, but that faith was based on his core belief that God was in control. He trusted that God held the universe in his hand.

In short, Elijah understood that God knows best—and he acted accordingly.

Do we?

1. Think about this last question. What are some of the ways God has blessed you, protected you, or opened important doors for you at different periods of your life?

Time Period	Major Ways God Acted on Your Behalf
During childhood	
As a teen	
As a young adult	
In the past ten years	

2. It's a safe bet that most of us would say God knows best about our lives, our needs, and our choices. But our actions often counter those statements. What is the hardest for you to do when it comes to actually *acting* as if God knows what is best for your life?

When my daughters were old enough to learn to drive a car, I chose to be their instructor. Other parents less prone to masochism enroll their teenagers in a driver's education class. Not this dad. I took on the task myself. We bought the training videos and studied the training books and then, on a day that left

Denalyn praying like Elijah, we climbed into the car, daughter at the wheel prepared for her maiden voyage.

Before telling her to start the engine, I gave her a spiel that went something like this: "At some point today I'm going to tell you to do something that will make no sense. A voice in your head will tell you to do something different. But you will need to trust me. You are driving; I am directing. If I say 'Change lanes,' you need to change lanes. If I say 'Slow down,' you need to slow down. Don't listen to the voice in your head. Listen to the voice of your dad. Will you?"

Will we?

The promises of God glitter like diamonds on the pages of Scripture. Will we gather them? Claim them? Delight in them? Pursue them?[20]

3. When was the last time you remember God directing you to do something that you didn't understand? (Perhaps this was through the Bible, through the inner voice of the Holy Spirit, or through the wise counsel of others.) How did you respond?

4. "The promises of God glitter like diamonds on the pages of Scripture." Which of those promises of God have been especially meaningful in your past? Which are you counting on for the future?

> 3 Trust in the LORD and do good;
> dwell in the land and enjoy safe pasture.
> 4 Take delight in the LORD,
> and he will give you the desires of your heart.
> 5 Commit your way to the LORD;
> trust in him and he will do this:
> 6 He will make your righteous reward shine like the dawn,
> your vindication like the noonday sun.
>
> PSALM 37:3-6

5. Notice the connection David makes in this psalm between belief and action: "*Trust* in the LORD and *do good*" (verse 3). How should trust and action be tied together in a believer's life? How does your trust in God motivate you to obey him and "do good"?

6. David also writes that you should "commit your way to the LORD" (verse 5). Where do you have an opportunity this week to demonstrate trust in God and truly commit your way to him? What action will you take based on that trust?

STUDY 2

GOD UNDERSTANDS

You're making your way down the road. Maybe you're listening to music or just admiring the scenery as it rolls along outside. Then you hear a soft beep and see a light on the dashboard. You're low on gas. Depending on the size of your tank and the efficiency of your vehicle, you can drive between thirty and sixty miles before you'll be officially empty.

Now, you have some options at this point.

Well, really, you have two options. The first is to heed the light, find a gas station, and fill 'er up. The second option is to ignore the alarm and just keep going. No filling station. No fuel. No concern about the inevitable collapse.

Let's say you chose that second option. You might try to encourage your vehicle to keep going despite its lack of fuel: "You can do this! You're a superstar." Or you could offer some advice: "The gas tank is a limit imposed on you by an unjust system. Don't let it define what you're capable of achieving." Or you might try a bit of tough love: "There's nothing wrong with you. Quit focusing on the negative. Snap out of it and be more positive."

Would any of those methods keep you moving down the road? Of course not. The warning light on your car's dashboard is alerting you to a problem that must be solved—an emptiness that must be filled.

There's a similar dynamic at play when men and women experience physical, mental, and emotional emptiness. It may be a clinical diagnosis of depression, or it may be a harder-to-define season of sadness, emptiness, grief, or pain. But whatever the root cause, it's undeniable that huge percentages of our population are trying to talk themselves or wish themselves or encourage themselves out of a real problem that needs real solutions.

Unfortunately, this tendency is prevalent in the church. Christians often think, *I shouldn't feel this sadness when I'm saved. I wouldn't be depressed if I were a better believer. I dare not have doubts after all that God has done for me.*

The reality is far more complex. And as you've already seen in this week's teaching, the issue of depression is something that the prophet Elijah experienced. Yes, even the man of unbreakable courage ran empty and felt run-down.

Thankfully, God understood.

And, thankfully for us, God still understands.

1. Times of grief, sadness, or depression can be difficult to understand. Use the space below to describe what you experienced during an especially heavy season of your life. (Consider sketching a picture, writing down memories, or recording key words.)

2. Depression and mental health issues have become prevalent within our culture over recent years. There has also been a greater awareness of those types of needs. How would you summarize our society's preferred methods for handling those issues?

3. Read Psalm 42:1–11. This passage is known as a *psalm of lament* because it expresses deep spiritual thirst, discouragement, and a feeling of separation from God.

What longing does the psalmist express in verses 1–4?

What does the psalmist choose to remember in verses 5–8?

What feelings of discouragement does he voice in verses 9–10?

What is the psalmist's closing challenge to himself in verse 11?

We'd expect Elijah to take a stand against Jezebel's implacability, to say to her what Saint Chrysostom said to the Empress Eudoxia: "Tell her that I fear nothing but sin." But, no, Elijah was so scared he made a run for it. He re-entered the driving storm and trudged his way a hundred miles across the hills of Samaria. . . .

We should stop and thank God for telling us this story. Seasons of sadness come to the most courageous saints. Did they not come to Christ? "While Jesus was here on earth, he offered prayers and pleadings, with a loud cry and tears, to the one who could rescue him from death" (Hebrews 5:7 NLT). . . .

If tears streaked the cheeks of Jesus, dare we feel shame when tears leave a trail on ours? Tough times happen to God's people. A sagging spirit is not a sign of a fragile faith. Let this example convey the truth: God has not given up on you. God has not abandoned you. You may be hard on yourself. But God? He responds to you in the way he responded to despondent Elijah.[21]

4. Look again at 1 Kings 19:11–18 to see how God responded to Elijah's despair. What specifically did God provide for his prophet in that moment?

5. Elijah felt that he was all alone. He was asking, like the psalmist, "Why have you forgotten me?" (Psalm 42:9). What did God reveal to Elijah to let him know he was *not* alone? What new task did the Lord give that would help him?

> 39 Jesus went out as usual to the Mount of Olives, and his disciples followed him. 40 On reaching the place, he said to them, "Pray that you will not fall into temptation." 41 He withdrew about a stone's throw beyond them, knelt down and prayed, 42 "Father, if you are willing, take this cup from me; yet not my will, but yours be done." 43 An angel from heaven appeared to him and strengthened him. 44 And being in anguish, he prayed more earnestly, and his sweat was like drops of blood falling to the ground.
>
> LUKE 22:39–44

6. Even Jesus felt the weight of emotions as he considered the task that lay ahead of him. As his follower, what steps can you take to be supportive, encouraging, and helpful when your loved ones walk through seasons of sadness?

STUDY 3

GOD SPEAKS

If you are a dog owner, or at least a friend of one, you know that most canines aren't fans of storms. When the winds blow, they whine. When the thunder booms, they dive for cover. When this happens, these panicked pups don't need a motivational speech or an inspirational sermon. They just need a few words of comfort and kindness.

"There, there. I'm with you. It'll be okay."

Now, there are some folks who find that silly. "What's the point of talking to your dog? You know they can't talk back."

That's true. You can't hold a conversation with a dog. They won't ask you about your day or offer you their opinions. They won't use words to request a second serving of dinner. (They prefer barks and howls.) Still, dog owners talk to their pets. And when thunder and lightning are in play, they need to hear the reassuring sound of their master's voice.

The same is true with God. We need to hear the sound of our Master's voice. Thankfully . . . amazingly . . . wonderfully—God offers that voice. He speaks not just *to* us but *with* us. When the storm rolls in and we want nothing more than to duck our heads and hope all the trouble goes away, God is there to say, "I'm with you. It'll be okay."

Elijah experienced the wonder of hearing God's voice in a physical way. When he was inside the cave at Horeb, a wind howled across the mountain that was strong enough to break stone. But the wind wasn't God's method of communication. Then came an earthquake and a fire. But neither was God's speech. Finally, Elijah heard "a gentle whisper" (1 Kings 19:12).

The prophet recognized that voice. "When Elijah heard it, he pulled his cloak over his face and went out and stood at the mouth of the cave" (verse 13). Elijah walked into the storm to have a chat with his Creator. What a miraculous moment!

Except . . . God speaking to us isn't all that unusual. He speaks to us every day through various means. Just think about this for a moment. The Lord of all things takes the time to shoot the breeze with you and me. He hears what we say. He listens. And he responds. We have the privilege of conversing with the Creator whenever we choose—even in the storms.

(Okay, especially in the storms!)

1. Read Hebrews 4:12 and 2 Timothy 3:16–17. One of the ways God speaks to us is through *special revelation*, which is the Bible. God has revealed key insights about his nature, his values, and his character throughout the pages of his Word.

What do you learn about the Word of God in Hebrews 4:12?

What is God's Word effective in doing according to 2 Timothy 3:16–17?

How has your approach to engaging the Bible developed over your lifetime?

> 1 The heavens declare the glory of God;
> the skies proclaim the work of his hands.
> 2 Day after day they pour forth speech;
> night after night they reveal knowledge.
> 3 They have no speech, they use no words;
> no sound is heard from them.
> 4 Yet their voice goes out into all the earth,
> their words to the ends of the world.
> In the heavens God has pitched a tent for the sun.
> 5 It is like a bridegroom coming out of his chamber,
> like a champion rejoicing to run his course.
> 6 It rises at one end of the heavens
> and makes its circuit to the other;
> nothing is deprived of its warmth.
>
> PSALM 19:1–6

2. God also speaks to us through *general revelation*, which includes the natural world and creation. Underline the imagery David uses in this psalm to show how God speaks to us. When has nature helped you connect with God in a meaningful way?

3. Read Matthew 10:18–20. God also speaks to us through *the Holy Spirit*. The Spirit lives in us and talks with us, including in those moments when we pray. In your experience, what most helps you hear the guidance of the Holy Spirit in your mind and heart?

4. Read 1 Samuel 3:1–10. Of course, God can also choose to speak *audibly* to his people. Why do you think God chose this approach when speaking with Samuel?

5. God called to Samuel three times before Eli recognized it was the Lord who was speaking. What in your life might be making it difficult to hear God speaking to you?

No lecture. No critique. No sermon. No finger-pointing or tongue-lashing. God comes kindly in the shadows. Soft as a flute solo. Tender as a mother's touch on the cheek of a tear-streaked child.

Such a tender restoration. This is the balm needed for the wounded soul. The strong fist of God was needed at Carmel. But the soothing touch of God was needed for Elijah's season of sadness.

Is God whispering to you? We look for God to come in the dramatic rolls of thunder. And he does, but he also comes as a Bethlehem babe, a descending dove, and a kind shepherd.[22]

6. Jesus said, "My sheep listen to my voice; I know them, and they follow me" (John 10:27). Jesus indeed speaks to us—but we must learn to recognize his voice.

When was the last time you were confident that God spoke to you directly?

How did you know it was God speaking to you?

How did you respond when you heard God's voice?

CATCH UP AND READ AHEAD

Connect with a fellow group member this week and discuss some of the key insights from this session. Use any of the following prompts to help guide your discussion.

- What were some of the emotions you experienced while working through this session? What do you think caused those emotions?
- When was the last time you remember God directing you to do something you didn't understand? How did you respond?
- As a follower of Jesus, what steps can you take to be supportive, encouraging, and helpful when loved ones walk through seasons of sadness?
- What are some of the ways that you have sensed God speaking to you in your life? What helps you to be still and hear his voice?
- "The street named Service is the surest path out of sadness."[23] How are you making acts of service a regular part of your worship to God?

Use this time to go back and complete any of the study and reflection questions from previous days that you weren't able to finish. Make a note below of any revelations you've had and reflect on any growth or personal insights you've gained.

Read chapters 9–10 in *Unbreakable Courage* before the next group gathering. Use the space below to note anything in those chapters that stands out to you or encourages you.

WEEK 5 *at a Glance*

THIS WEEK'S READING	Chapters 9–10 in *Unbreakable Courage*
GROUP MEETING	Read the Welcome and Connect with the group (page 95) Watch the video and take notes (pages 96–97) Discuss the questions that follow (page 98) Respond to the teaching and Close (pages 99–100)
PERSONAL STUDIES: Study 1 Study 2 Study 3	 "When God Gets Angry" (pages 102–105) "No Hiding from God" (pages 106–109) "The Cycle Continues" (pages 110–112)
CATCH UP AND READ AHEAD (BEFORE WEEK 6 MEETING)	Connect with someone in your group Complete any unfinished personal studies (page 113)
NEXT WEEK'S READING	Chapters 11–12 in *Unbreakable Courage*

SESSION FIVE

DON'T KISS THE SNAKE

Ahab said to Elijah, "So you have found me, my enemy!" "I have found you," he answered, "because you have sold yourself to do evil in the eyes of the Lord. *He says, 'I am going to bring disaster on you. I will wipe out your descendants and cut off from Ahab every last male in Israel—slave or free. I will make your house like that of Jeroboam son of Nebat and that of Baasha son of Ahijah, because you have aroused my anger and have caused Israel to sin.'"*

1 KINGS 21:20-22

Elijah confronts Ahab and
flees to the Kerith Ravine
(1 Kings 17:1–6)

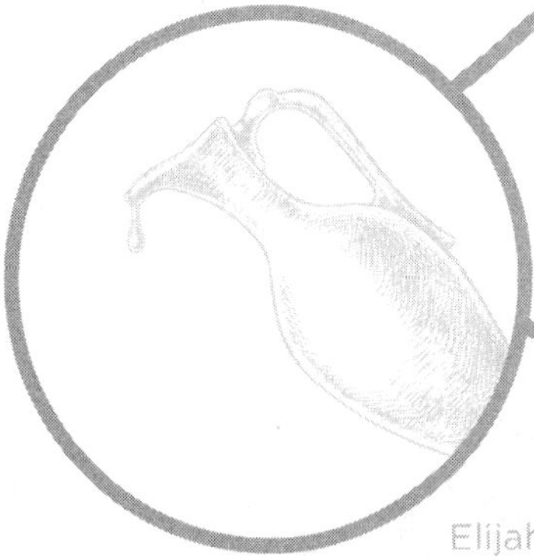

Elijah goes to the widow's
home at Zarephath
(1 Kings 17:7–24)

Elijah confronts the false
prophets at Mount Carmel
(1 Kings 18:16–40)

The drought ends and
Elijah flees to Horeb
(1 Kings 18:41–19:18)

Elijah confronts King Ahab
and his son Ahaziah
(1 Kings 21:1–28; 2 Kings 2:1–18)

WELCOME | READ ON YOUR OWN

David Blaine is a world-famous illusionist (or magician to the layperson) who has stunned his fans for decades by pulling off what seems to be impossible. Back in 2025, however, Blaine took on a different assignment. He traveled around the world for National Geographic to document performers who go to great lengths and take great risks to master their crafts.

During one segment, Blaine traveled to Southeast Asia for what he described as the most stressful kiss of his life. It was stressful because he kissed a *snake*. A king cobra to be precise—the world's longest venomous snake. The whole event was controlled and monitored by a professional handler . . . but there are only so many safety checks you can make when you plan to get up close and personal with a deadly serpent.[24]

David Blaine kissed that particular snake without being harmed. Thank goodness. Still, there is a reason his series is called "Do Not Attempt." In this case, the lesson to be learned is do not attempt what David Blaine attempted. *Don't kiss the snake.*

What do we mean by this? Don't get close to what you know to be dangerous. Specifically, don't get close to sin. There are far too many people today who enjoy the process of cozying up to sinful choices and immoral habits. They like the thrill. They like the pleasure. They feel that they are reveling in freedom by dancing with danger.

In reality, those who take such risks are guaranteed to get bitten sooner or later. (Probably way sooner than they expect.) That's because sin carries consequences. You could even say that sin *creates* consequences.

We get what we deserve. We reap what we sow. King Ahab found that out the hard way, as we'll see in this session. So did his son Ahaziah.

Don't follow in their footsteps. Don't kiss the snake.

CONNECT | 10 MINUTES

Get this session started by discussing one of these questions:

- What is the most interesting interaction you've ever had with a snake?

— or —

- What have you seen in the news this week that confirms the reality of evil?

WATCH | 25 MINUTES

Now watch the video for this session. Below is an outline of the key points covered during the teaching. Record any key concepts that stand out to you.

OUTLINE

I. We often play with temptation as if it were a pet or something we can control.

A. We have an enemy of our souls, Satan, and we do ourselves no favor by dismissing him as a myth.

B. God commands us to not give Satan a foothold in our lives (see Ephesians 4:27).

C. Satan's aim is always to "steal and kill and destroy" (John 10:10).

II. Elijah took evil seriously, even though the culture around him did not.

A. Ahab and Jezebel continued to rebel against God and lead the people astray.

B. The final straw came when they had a man killed so they could steal his vineyard.

C. The couple's inability to see the value in human life was diabolical, disgusting, and demonic.

D. A steadfast faith includes a healthy respect for God's righteous anger.

III. God demonstrated his mercy when Ahab repented.

A. Elijah's verdict against Ahab and his family shook the king—and he repented.

B. God responded to Ahab's gesture of humility by postponing the verdict.

C. We can't make the mistake, however, of believing God's patience is his ignorance.

D. God's justice ultimately came because Ahab and Jezebel continued in their sin.

IV. We must take evil seriously if we want to live for God in a faithless world.

A. When Ahaziah came to power, he maintained the evil and idolatry of his parents.

B. Elijah did not shy away from standing up to Ahaziah's sin and declaring God's judgment again him.

C. The same God who empowered Elijah will empower us to confront evil.

D. We have weapons Satan cannot match—prayer, worship, and the Word.

E. We can refuse to cavort with the enemy and, instead, choose to be strong and courageous in the Lord.

NOTES

DISCUSS | 35 MINUTES

Discuss what you just watched by answering the following questions.

1. Think about the concept of "kissing the snake"—keeping ourselves in proximity to temptation or sin. How does the culture encourage us to cozy up with what we know is wrong? What are some specific examples of this that you see in today's world?

2. Ask someone to read aloud Ephesians 4:22–27. What does it mean to "put off your old self"? What does it mean to "give the devil a foothold" in your life?

3. Now ask someone to read 1 Kings 21:20–26. Ahab and Jezebel had "bought into the business of evil" (verse 20 MSG). When you reflect on everything we've covered in this study, what chances had God given them to change? Why do you think, after his initial repentance, Ahab went back to the business of doing evil?

4. We would like to believe that the death of King Ahab brought Israel to a widespread return to the Lord. But alas, Ahaziah was a chip off the old demonic block. How did Elijah demonstrate unbreakable courage in his confrontation with this particular ungodly king? Where do you see an opportunity right now to stand courageously for good in your community?

5. Paul wrote that the weapons we have at our disposal "have divine power to demolish strongholds" (2 Corinthians 10:4). Which of these weapons—such as prayer, worship, and the Word—are you using today to battle against the enemy? Which of these weapons do you need to pick up or wield more effectively in the fight?

RESPOND | 10 MINUTES

Generations of Christians have recognized the book of James as one of the most practical and helpful epistles of the New Testament. The apostle tackles many subjects in letter, but he does so with a compactness and an efficiency that really pack a punch.

James wrote to the church during a season of intense persecution from several sides. The Jewish leaders in many cities were actively persecuting members of the early church, both by excommunicating them from the larger Jewish community and by actively attacking Christians—including putting them to death. Likewise, the authority of the Roman Empire had begun to swing against Christians, singling them out for all manner of punishment and cruelty.

That being the case, it's helpful to see what James had to say about this topic of standing courageously in the face of evil:

> 6 But he gives us more grace. That is why Scripture says: "God opposes the proud but shows favor to the humble." 7 Submit yourselves, then, to God. Resist the devil, and he will flee from you. 8 Come near to God and he will come near to you. Wash your hands, you sinners, and purify your hearts, you double-minded. 9 Grieve, mourn and wail. Change your laughter to mourning and your joy to gloom. 10 Humble yourselves before the Lord, and he will lift you up.
>
> JAMES 4:6-10

Take a few moments to reread this passage and make a list of all the commands that are given. What promises are included with those commands?

In your experience, what does it look like on a practical level to "resist the devil"? How are followers of Jesus to actively resist the devil as part of their daily lives?

CLOSE | 10 MINUTES

When the time comes to close this session, spend some time acknowledging your tendency (and the tendencies of every person) to remain close to sin and sinful habits even though you know they are harmful. Affirm the reality of evil in this world and ask for the Holy Spirit to fill each of you with strength and unbreakable courage so you can stand firm on truth, goodness, and justice. Use the space below to write down any requests that are raised so that you and your group members can pray about them in the upcoming week.

Name	Request

SESSION FIVE

PERSONAL STUDY

When God appeared to Moses at Mount Sinai, he declared, "The Lord, the compassionate and gracious God, slow to anger, abounding in love and faithfulness, maintaining love to thousands, and forgiving wickedness, rebellion and sin." But in the next breath, he added, "Yet he does not leave the guilty unpunished; he punishes the children and their children for the sin of the parents to the third and fourth generation" (Exodus 34:6–7). Ahab experienced God's mercy (when he repented) and God's justice (when he continued to do evil). In this week's personal study, you will explore the reality of evil, God's wrath against it, and his command for his followers to refuse to "kiss the snake," so to speak. Continue to write down your responses to the questions to share with the group at the next meeting. If you are reading *Unbreakable Courage* alongside this study, first review chapters 9–10 of the book.

STUDY 1

WHEN GOD GETS ANGRY

"You wouldn't like me when I'm angry." We all know where that catchphrase is from. Okay, most of us know. It's from the Incredible Hulk—the hugely muscled, loud, destructive green rage-monster who serves as the alter ego for the mild-mannered scientist Dr. Bruce Banner. When Banner gets angry, he transforms from a man into a monster.

This is typically how we view anger—as an out-of-control emotion. In our minds, a person who is angry is going down a harmful path. This means that people who are angry can't be trusted, because they're not acting logically.

Anger is scary. It's even worse when people are overwhelmed by more intense forms of anger, such as rage, fury, and wrath.

Perhaps it's this particular view of anger that makes us hesitant to connect that emotion with God. We don't like thinking of God as angry. We don't like talking about him as vengeful or wrathful or furious or enraged. The problem is that the Bible does describe God in those terms.

The psalmist wrote, "The Lord is a God who avenges. O God who avenges, shine forth" (Psalm 94:1). Jesus said, "Whoever believes in the Son has eternal life, but whoever rejects the Son will not see life, for God's wrath remains on them" (John 3:36). Paul wrote, "God's anger is shown from heaven against all the evil and wrong things people do. By their own evil lives they hide the truth" (Romans 1:18 NCV).

As much as we rightly understand that love, mercy, and compassion are critical elements of God's character, we must recognize that anger and wrath are as well. That's because God is just—and anger is the just response when holiness is exposed to evil.

Now, we need to be clear. When the Bible speaks of God's anger, it is nearly always anger on behalf of the oppressed. The unjustified ill-treatment of others stirs up God's wrath. Especially when people prey on others who cannot protect or defend themselves.

Thankfully, God is not like the Incredible Hulk. His anger and wrath do not cause him to lose control and lash out indiscriminately. No, God's anger is a righteous rage. It is a holy, controlled, and purposeful response to injustice, sin, and evil. It seeks to restore or to prevent further evil. God's anger is part of his character—and it is loving.

Let's dig deeper into what that reality means for our lives.

1. To what degree do the following situations cause you to feel significant anger?

When your spouse gets after you for something you forgot to do

1 2 3 4 5 6 7 8 9 10
[not much] [quite a lot]

When coworkers forget to do something you asked them to do

1 2 3 4 5 6 7 8 9 10
[not much] [quite a lot]

When your children do something you told them not to do

1 2 3 4 5 6 7 8 9 10
[not much] [quite a lot]

When someone cuts you off on the road

1 2 3 4 5 6 7 8 9 10
[not much] [quite a lot]

When your favorite sports team makes mistake after mistake

1 2 3 4 5 6 7 8 9 10
[not much] [quite a lot]

When you listen to the national news

1 2 3 4 5 6 7 8 9 10
[not much] [quite a lot]

2. Think back to the latest few times you felt really angry. Do you typically maintain control of your words in those moments—or are you more like the Hulk?

> Actions have consequences. God's authority can be flaunted for only so long and then "the wicked are trapped by their own deeds" (Psalm 9:16 NLT).
>
> God is just.
>
> We speak often of God's love. Well, we should. The tenderness of our Maker toward his children is the great lighthouse on the shore. We set our gaze on it and find our way home. We are right to major in God's love.
>
> But we are wrong to minimize his judgment. Unbreakable courage and steadfast faith include a healthy respect for God's righteous anger. To be clear: God is not an angry God. He is not like an eruptive husband who beats his wife, an exacting boss who cannot be pleased, or an abusive mother who delights in stirring up fear in her children.[25]

3. Read Psalm 7:6-9 and Deuteronomy 32:35. Do you feel uncomfortable with the thought of God—who is all-powerful—experiencing emotions like anger? What about a God who says, "It is mine to avenge; I will repay"? Explain your answer.

4. Read Proverbs 3:5-6. One reason we don't feel comfortable with an angry God is because we lack trust—a topic we've discussed throughout this study. What are some of the main obstacles hindering your ability to trust God in *all* circumstances?

[17] Do not repay anyone evil for evil. Be careful to do what is right in the eyes of everyone. [18] If it is possible, as far as it depends on you, live at peace with everyone. [19] Do not take revenge, my dear friends, but leave room for God's wrath, for it is written: "It is mine to avenge; I will repay," says the Lord. [20] On the contrary:

> "If your enemy is hungry, feed him;
> if he is thirsty, give him something to drink.
> In doing this, you will heap burning coals on his head."

[21] Do not be overcome by evil, but overcome evil with good.

ROMANS 12:17–21

5. Accepting the reality of *God's* anger does not mean we embrace our own *human* anger. What does Paul say in this passage about how followers of Jesus are to live?

6. Paul says we should not try to step into God's place when it comes to vengeance. Why do you think God commands his followers not to take revenge? What does it mean to not allow yourself to "be overcome by evil, but overcome evil with good" (verse 21)?

STUDY 2

NO HIDING FROM GOD

In this week's group time, you briefly touched on a confrontation between Ahab and a vineyard owner named Naboth. Let's dig a bit deeper into that story, because it reveals another important reality we must keep in mind when we consider the reality of evil.

"Some time later there was an incident involving a vineyard belonging to Naboth the Jezreelite" (1 Kings 21:1). Naboth is introduced as the owner of a vineyard in the town of Jezreel. Apparently, he owned a particularly nice vineyard, because King Ahab wanted it. He desired it as part of his real estate holdings and offered to buy the land from Naboth.

This is where things get a little complicated. In ancient Israel, property was supposed to remain within specific families. When Joshua and the Israelites conquered the promised land, God divided up the territory among the twelve tribes but also among the major families within each tribe. Those families were to steward their land in perpetuity. Meaning, they weren't supposed to sell it. Not only that, but if someone found themselves in financial trouble and *had* to sell their land, other members of that family were to redeem it during the next Year of Jubilee. This was all part of the Mosaic Law.

This means Naboth wasn't *allowed* to sell his vineyard. Doing so would have broken God's law. Of course, Ahab wasn't worried about that. Neither was Jezebel. In fact, the queen was so sick of her husband's moping that she arranged to have Naboth falsely accused of heresy—and then put to death in the street. In her mind, this was an easy way to solve Ahab's problem and make sure the king could buy whatever land he wanted.

The problem was that neither Ahab nor Jezebel could hide their actions from God. He was watching. He is *always* watching.

When Elijah showed up at the grand opening of the king's new winery, he said, "I have found you . . . because you have sold yourself to do evil in the eyes of the LORD" (verse 20).

This is what we must remember about the reality of evil—that God will always find those who engage in it. Of course, that truth should convict us in our own battles against sin. But it should also comfort us when we feel as if all the wicked people are getting away with their crimes. Because they're not—and they won't. God will bring justice.

1. Read 1 Kings 21:1–16. How would you describe Ahab and Jezebel's attitudes toward people in this story? How would you describe their attitude toward sin?

How would you describe Ahab's attitude when he couldn't get what he wanted?

How would you describe Ahab and Jezebel's attitudes toward people in this story?

How would you describe Ahab and Jezebel's attitude toward sin?

2. Read Numbers 32:23. There are many people today who seem to be getting away with murder (so to speak). What types of crimes, rackets, or schemes make you feel especially frustrated when they go unpunished? What does God say about sin in this verse?

> [30] Then Jehu went to Jezreel. When Jezebel heard about it, she put on eye makeup, arranged her hair and looked out of a window. [31] As Jehu entered the gate, she asked, "Have you come in peace, you Zimri, you murderer of your master?"
>
> [32] He looked up at the window and called out, "Who is on my side? Who?" Two or three eunuchs looked down at him. [33] "Throw her down!" Jehu said. So they threw her down, and some of her blood spattered the wall and the horses as they trampled her underfoot.
>
> [34] Jehu went in and ate and drank. "Take care of that cursed woman," he said, "and bury her, for she was a king's daughter." [35] But when they went out to bury her, they found nothing except her skull, her feet and her hands. [36] They went back and told Jehu, who said, "This is the word of the LORD that he spoke through his servant Elijah the Tishbite: On the plot of ground at Jezreel dogs will devour Jezebel's flesh. [37] Jezebel's body will be like dung on the ground in the plot at Jezreel, so that no one will be able to say, 'This is Jezebel.'"
>
> 2 KINGS 9:30-37

3. This passage describes the gruesome end of Jezebel's life, which happened after Ahab and their son were also killed. How did Elijah's prophecy about Jezebel come to pass?

4. Read Galatians 6:7–8. Jezebel's death represents God's judgment on life lived in unrepentant rebellion. What does Paul say about the type of "seeds" we can sow in this life? What are the consequences of the particular seeds we choose to sow?

The truth is, we are all guilty. We have not murdered like Mao Zedong or abused like Jezebel, but each one of us has fallen short of our intended level of holiness. We deserve God's wrath. Yet, "Jesus . . . rescues us from the coming wrath" (1 Thessalonians 1:10). On the cross he endured the judgment against our sin for us. Through Christ, we escape the verdict.

Christ offers us a safe place—a place where God's righteous wrath has already passed.

The Naboth story, be it ever so unpleasant, is important. It illustrates a justice that comforts the wounded and warns the wicked. Do you long for justice to be served? It will be. Do you think your sin is unnoticed? It's not. Let God's justice have its desired impact. Let it calm you, convict you, or both.[26]

5. Paul wrote, "There is no one righteous, not even one" (Romans 3:10). James said, "Whoever keeps the whole law and yet stumbles at just one point is guilty of breaking all of it" (James 2:10). It's easy to point at Ahab and Jezebel and call them wicked. But what do these verses say about *every* person's failings before our holy God?

6. "Jesus . . . rescues us from the coming wrath" (1 Thessalonians 1:10). To be a follower of Jesus is to be safe from God's wrath poured out against sin and evil. How would you explain that safety to someone who has never heard about salvation?

STUDY 3

THE CYCLE CONTINUES

By this point, you've probably had enough of hearing about Ahab and Jezebel. But we have to spend a little time talking about their son Ahaziah. *Little* is the operative word here, because the Bible doesn't actually have a lot to say about him.

Here is his grand introduction in Scripture: "He did evil in the eyes of the LORD, because he followed the ways of his father and mother and of Jeroboam son of Nebat, who caused Israel to sin. He served and worshiped Baal and aroused the anger of the Lord, the God of Israel, just as his father had done" (1 Kings 22:52–53).

Not exactly encouraging. And it gets worse. Here's how the next chapter starts: "Now Ahaziah had fallen through the lattice of his upper room in Samaria and injured himself. So he sent messengers, saying to them, 'Go and consult Baal-Zebub, the god of Ekron, to see if I will recover from this injury'" (2 Kings 1:2).

Think about this for a moment. Ahaziah was the prince when Elijah burst into the throne room to declare a drought—and the drought came to the land. He at least knew about the events when Elijah called down fire at the pinnacle of Mount Carmel, proving the superiority of God over Baal and Asherah. He witnessed the rain return right when God said it would happen.

In other words, Ahaziah had a front-row seat to the miracles of the one true God. Time and again, he witnessed Elijah's prophecies come true. Yet when he became injured, he sent someone to ask *Baal*—a false god—whether he would be healed.

In spite of all the evidence, young Ahaziah chose to kiss the snake. He chose to worship idols rather than submit himself to the Lord of the universe. What a shame.

And what a shame that so many people make the same choice today. God has made every effort to show humanity the truth about himself. He has extended lifeline after lifeline in our direction, reaching out to us through the beauty of the natural world, the truth of Scripture, the power of miracles, and the long record of history. He even sent his only Son to die on a cross so that all people on the earth could be saved.

Yet many reject his love and choose idols instead. It's a tragedy every time—and one that carries eternal consequences.

1. How did you encounter the message of forgiveness and salvation through Jesus Christ? Use the space below to describe the moment you experienced a connection with God and became a new creation through him. (Write it down, draw a picture, or choose whatever method is most comfortable to you.)

2. Read Romans 1:18–23. How has God revealed himself to humanity? What does it mean that "people are without excuse" (verse 20) when it comes to knowing God?

3. Review Ahaziah's story in 2 Kings 1:1–18. Paul writes that people "exchanged the glory of the immortal God for images made to look like a mortal human being" (Romans 1:23). How was this true in Ahaziah's case? What were the consequences of Ahaziah's choice—for both him and his men—in seeking help from Baal instead of the living God?

4. Read 1 Corinthians 10:14–22. This group of Christian believers were not *technically* worshiping false gods, but they were eating food sacrificed to idols and participating in the pagan religious festivities in the city. How were these believers "kissing the snake," so to speak, when it came to engaging in these activities?

5. What does Paul mean when he says "you cannot drink the cup of the Lord and the cup of demons too" (verse 21)? How does that warning apply even to Christians today?

> The most insidious work of the devil is counterfeit religion. His deadliest attacks occur, not in casinos or gentleman's clubs, but in temples and sanctuaries and mosques. Why? Because the human heart longs to worship. It's the most natural thing in the world. God has "set eternity in the human heart" (Ecclesiastes 3:11), and our reach for the divine reflects our longing for him. The devilish cunning of counterfeit religion is that it mixes in just enough truth to make the lie all the stronger. Satan sold a bag of lies to Ahaziah. The king saw a false god, Baal-Zebub, as an attractive and sure solution to his calamity. A bald-faced rejection of Jehovah.[27]

6. The human heart longs to worship. As the famed preacher Charles Spurgeon wrote, "Nothing teaches us about the preciousness of the Creator as much as when we learn the emptiness of everything else."[28] How have you found this to be true in your life?

CATCH UP AND READ AHEAD

Connect with a fellow group member this week and discuss some of the key insights from this session. Use any of the following prompts to help guide your discussion.

- What is your biggest takeaway from this week's discussion on not "kissing the snake"? Why does that point stand out to you?
- Do you feel uncomfortable with the thought of God, who is all-powerful, experiencing anger—even wrath? Explain your response.
- What are some of the ways that people try to hide their actions from God? What is the result when we don't treat sin as serious?
- Why do you think God is so adamant that we worship nothing else but him? What happens when we turn to worldly things to meet our needs?
- What convicted you the most in this session? What is one step you will take this week to avoid kissing the snake?

Use this time to go back and complete any of the study and reflection questions from previous days that you weren't able to finish. Make a note below of any revelations you've had and reflect on any growth or personal insights you've gained.

Read chapters 11–12 in *Unbreakable Courage* before the next group gathering. Use the space below to note anything in those chapters that stands out to you or encourages you.

WEEK 6 *at a Glance*

THIS WEEK'S READING	Chapters 11–12 in *Unbreakable Courage*
GROUP MEETING	Read the Welcome and Connect with the group (page 117) Watch the video and take notes (pages 118–119) Discuss the questions that follow (page 120) Respond to the teaching and Close (pages 121–122)
PERSONAL STUDIES: Study 1 Study 2 Study 3	 "All According to Plan" (pages 124–127) "In Our Father's Hands" (pages 128–132) "The God of Israel Lives!" (pages 133–136)
WRAP UP	Connect with someone in your group Complete any unfinished personal studies (page 137) Talk with your group about the next study that you want to go through together

SESSION SIX

WAITING ON THE WHIRLWIND

As [Elijah and Elisha] were walking along and talking together, suddenly a chariot of fire and horses of fire appeared and separated the two of them, and Elijah went up to heaven in a whirlwind. Elisha saw this and cried out, "My father! My father! The chariots and horsemen of Israel!" And Elisha saw him no more. Then he took hold of his garment and tore it in two.

2 KINGS 2:11-12

Elijah confronts Ahab and flees to the Kerith Ravine (1 Kings 17:1–6)

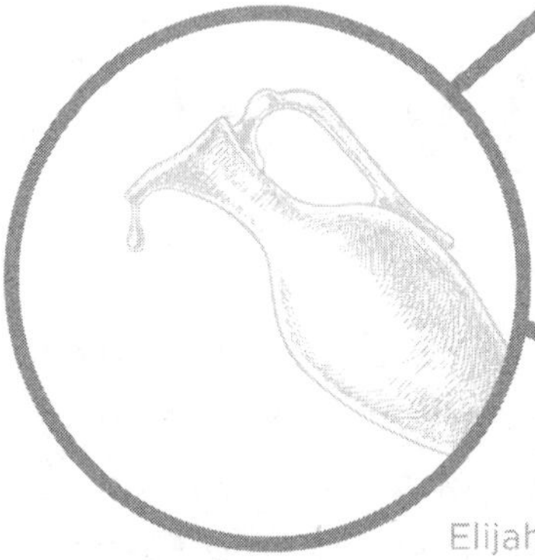

Elijah goes to the widow's home at Zarephath (1 Kings 17:7–24)

Elijah confronts the false prophets at Mount Carmel (1 Kings 18:16–40)

The drought ends and Elijah flees to Horeb (1 Kings 18:41–19:18)

Elijah confronts King Ahab and his son Ahaziah (1 Kings 21:1–28; 2 Kings 2:1–18)

Elijah is taken up into heaven in a whirlwind (2 Kings 2:1–14)

WELCOME | READ ON YOUR OWN

Batman has Robin. Garfield has Odie. Frodo Baggins has Samwise Gamgee. Texas has the rest of the United States. (Sorry, couldn't resist.)

What am I talking about? Sidekicks. Most of the best characters in the entertainment world would fall a bit flat if they had to carry a story or hog the spotlight all by themselves. But when you put them side by side with a trusty subordinate . . . they shine.

Somewhere near the end of Elijah's prophetic ministry, the Lord told him to call a young man named Elisha as his assistant. Now, to be fair, Elisha wasn't a sidekick—he wasn't a side character whose main point was to offer a little comic relief and make the main character look good. No, Elisha was more of a protégé. He was there to serve his master, learn all that he could, and one day step into Elijah's shoes.

Which is exactly what happened.

Imagine everything Elisha must have seen and heard while walking in his master's footsteps. Miracles. Confrontations. Worship. Imagine everything the younger man would have learned just by sitting at his master's feet. Yes, I'm sure there were challenges of many kinds, but the opportunities must have been amazing.

And then, sooner than Elisha hoped, the day arrived when Elijah was summoned home. The old prophet had reached the end of the road, but he didn't cower in fear or anxiety. Rather, he spent his final moments training the next generation of leaders. He then faced the end of his life with the same unbreakable courage that had marked his ministry.

We will conclude this study by exploring that final day for Elijah the prophet—and all the miraculous events that went with it. As we do, let's look for opportunities to apply Elijah's courage and his steadfast faith to whatever challenge we see on the horizon—even including our final steps on the path that we've walked for so long.

CONNECT | 10 MINUTES

Get this session started by discussing one of these questions:

- When have you had a surprising encounter with the natural world?

— or —

- What is your most striking memory from a funeral or a graveside service?

WATCH | 25 MINUTES

Now watch the video for this session. Below is an outline of the key points covered during the teaching. Record any key concepts that stand out to you.

OUTLINE

I. God promises to come at an unexpected hour and take us to our eternal home.

A. Since we don't know that new world, we aren't sure we want to go.

B. But we don't need to fear that future moment, because our God is a good Father.

II. Elijah began his story in a blaze of glory and exited in the same way.

A. Elijah's final day was spent in the company of his protégé Elisha.

B. Fellow prophets told Elisha that his master would be taken that day.

C. Elijah was visiting training grounds for future prophets in Bethel, Jericho, and the Jordan.

D. We don't know how Elijah responded to the news that his final day on earth had come.

E. Ultimately, a chariot of fire appeared, and Elijah was taken up to heaven in a whirlwind.

III. Elijah teaches us how to live with courage *and* how to face our final days with faith.

A. We all have a start date and an end date, known by God before we were born.

B. We cannot control our time of death, but we can control what we do with the time we're given.

C. Until we die or Jesus returns, we have work to do—beginning with the Great Commission.

IV. At the end of the day, what can we learn from Elijah's story?

A. We can be a beacon of uncompromised faith even if we are in the middle of a compromised generation.

B. We follow in Elijah's footsteps by believing what he believed—that the God of Israel lives!

C. Draw near to God. Keep believing and growing. Let your faith be steadfast in him.

NOTES

DISCUSS | 35 MINUTES

Discuss what you just watched by answering the following questions.

1. Ask someone to read 1 Corinthians 15:51–57. Death is a subject that most of us want to avoid, but we know that an "extraction" from this world is coming. Growing up, how was the subject of death dealt with in your family? What does Paul say about death in this passage—and what comfort does it bring to you as a follower of Christ?

2. Jesus, on the night before his death, told his disciples, "My Father's house has many rooms; if that were not so, would I have told you that I am going there to prepare a place for you?" (John 14:2). What comes to mind when you picture the "house" with "rooms" that Jesus is preparing for you? How does that imagery bring you hope?

3. Ask someone else to read 2 Kings 2:1–14 out loud. What is the significance of Elijah visiting Bethel, Jericho, and the Jordan regions on the last day of his life on earth? What are your impressions of Elisha based on his actions in this passage?

4. James said, "Life is like a mist. You can see it for a short time, but then it goes away" (James 4:14 NCV). You cannot control the inevitability of death, but you can decide what you will do between now and then. For those of us who are not prophets like Elijah, what does God expect from us as we live, work, play, and minister each day?

5. At the end of the day, what is *your* biggest takeaway from Elijah's life? What have you learned from his story that will help you to have unbreakable courage?

RESPOND | 10 MINUTES

Paul wrote that as a servant of Christ he had been in prison frequently, flogged severely, and "exposed to death again and again" (2 Corinthians 11:23). During one such imprisonment, likely in Rome, he wrote the letter of Philippians. Paul was under threat of death at the time and was scheduled to appear before an emperor known to despise followers of Jesus.

With the benefit of history, we know that Paul was released from jail—for a time. He went on to plant more churches and spread the gospel even farther throughout the known world. But at the time he wrote his letter to the Christians in Philippi, he had no idea what was going to happen. Would he live or die? Continue to serve or transition to heaven?

Paul's meditations on those two options have encouraged followers of Jesus for nearly two thousand years:

> [21] For to me, to live is Christ and to die is gain. [22] If I am to go on living in the body, this will mean fruitful labor for me. Yet what shall I choose? I do not know! [23] I am torn between the two: I desire to depart and be with Christ, which is better by far; [24] but it is more necessary for you that I remain in the body. [25] Convinced of this, I know that I will remain, and I will continue with all of you for your progress and joy in the faith, [26] so that through my being with you again your boasting in Christ Jesus will abound on account of me.
>
> PHILIPPIANS 1:21–26

What benefit did Paul see from being granted his freedom and allowed to continue his ministry? What benefit did he see if he ended up being martyred for his faith?

Paul referred to his work as "fruitful labor." What is your labor for God's kingdom here on earth? In other words, what is the work that God has set aside for you to accomplish?

CLOSE | 10 MINUTES

Conclude this session by celebrating the fact that God has prepared an eternal home for all his children. Affirm your desire to be a productive member of God's kingdom for whatever time he has granted you to be here on earth. Ask the Holy Spirit to imprint on your heart the lessons from Elijah's life that he wants you to learn and apply. Finally, for one last time in this study, use the space below to write down any requests that you and your group members have so you can pray about them in the weeks and months ahead.

Name	Request

SESSION SIX

PERSONAL STUDY

The life of Elijah is not a detailed story—nor is it one that covers dozens of pages in God's Word. As you have seen, he was born at a time in Israel's history when it was dangerous to be a prophet of God. For more than a century, the Israelites had mocked their heritage and engaged in idol worship, serving as tools of Satan. Elijah was a lightning bolt that streaked into biblical history to upset this order. His life blazed with faith and courage—and then, as suddenly as he had appeared, he was taken into heaven in a fiery chariot. In this final personal study, you will continue to reflect on the impact of Elijah's story and take a deeper look at God's appointed time for your life. As you work through these exercises, continue writing down your responses so you can share with others in your group. If you are reading *Unbreakable Courage* alongside this study, first review chapters 11–12 of the book.

STUDY 1

ALL ACCORDING TO PLAN

Mark Twain wrote, "The fear of death follows from the fear of life. A man who lives fully is prepared to die at any time."[29] It's a nice thought. But with all due respect to the great humorist, most of us are at least a little unsettled about the thought of death.

After all, we hear of tragedies every day. A doctor's diagnosis that strikes from out of the blue. A car accident that takes away someone all too soon. An act of nature that decimates an entire community. It's hard not to get a bit unnerved when we hear these kinds of stories. What if something unexpected crashes the party we call life?

Elijah understood what it meant to live under the threat of death. Think about all the times powerful people wanted to kill him. Remember what Obadiah, the palace administrator, said to him? "The king has searched every nation and kingdom on earth from end to end to find you" (1 Kings 18:10 NLT). Yet his efforts came to nothing. Elijah outlived him.

Queen Jezebel also vowed to kill God's prophet. She even sent a messenger to tell him in advance what she planned to do: "So let the gods do to me, and more also, if I do not make your life as the life of one of [the prophets of Baal] by tomorrow about this time" (19:2 NKJV). Once again, the promise fell flat. Elijah presided over her final days as well.

What about Ahaziah? Three times, he sent a captain with fifty soldiers to strike down Elijah. Two times, the captains and their men were consumed by fire from heaven. Only the common sense of the third captain prevented more soldiers from becoming charcoal.

Through it all, the prophet Elijah survived. He kept working year after year in service to God. He anointed kings. He called Elisha as his apprentice. He trained the next generation of prophets.

But then we read this verse: "Now the sons of the prophets who were at Bethel came out to Elisha, and said to him, 'Do you know that the LORD will take away your master from over you today?'" (2 Kings 2:3 NKJV). Somehow, word got out that Elijah had reached the end of the line. Which means God had already planned the end of that line—the prophet's final day. Which means nothing and nobody could have killed Elijah before God's appointed time.

The same is true for you. Don't fear the end that your good Father has arranged for you. Everything will happen according to his plan.

1. Read Psalm 139:13–18 and reflect on the idea that God has a specific plan for your life. How does it encourage you to know that all your days are ordained by him?

2. There are many fears that people have concerning death. Some of the most common are listed below. On a scale of 1 to 10, rank how each one weighs on your mind.

Fear of experiencing pain and suffering

1 2 3 4 5 6 7 8 9 10

[a little] [a lot]

Fear of not knowing what will happen in the afterlife

1 2 3 4 5 6 7 8 9 10

[a little] [a lot]

Fear of leaving loved ones behind (and what will happen to them)

1 2 3 4 5 6 7 8 9 10

[a little] [a lot]

Fear of leaving behind an unfinished or unfulfilled life

1 2 3 4 5 6 7 8 9 10

[a little] [a lot]

3. Think about the fear of leaving behind an unfulfilled life. When you look at Elijah's story in 2 Kings 2:1–6, what do you find the prophet doing on the last day of his life? How did Elijah make sure that he was enabling his ministry to continue on?

Dietrich Bonhoeffer earned Adolf Hitler's hatred for his involvement in the German resistance, including a plot to assassinate the führer. Eventually he was arrested and set to be executed. Bonhoeffer's exploits were the stuff of spy novels, but in truth, the man was simply a pastor. He stood against Hitler because he stood for Christ.

"Less than twenty-four hours before he left this world, Bonhoeffer performed the offices of a pastor. In the bright Schönberg schoolroom that was their cell, he held a small service."[30] Bonhoeffer used his final hours to encourage his brothers. Elijah traveled from city to city building up God's faithful.

May we be found doing the same. Serving. Loving. Teaching. Praying.[31]

4. Read John 13:1–17. Jesus knew "the hour had come for him to leave this world" (verse 1). Yet what did he do on the last night before his death? When you look at Jesus' example, what does it say about what you should be doing with your time on earth?

5. Isaiah proclaimed, "Trust in the LORD forever, for the LORD . . . is the Rock eternal" (Isaiah 26:4). It takes courage to trust God with the end of your life. When you feel afraid about death, what helps to reinforce your trust in God's good timing?

> [7] For none of us lives for ourselves alone, and none of us dies for ourselves alone. [8] If we live, we live for the Lord; and if we die, we die for the Lord. So, whether we live or die, we belong to the Lord. [9] For this very reason, Christ died and returned to life so that he might be the Lord of both the dead and the living.
>
> [10] You, then, why do you judge your brother or sister? Or why do you treat them with contempt? For we will all stand before God's judgment seat. . . .
>
> [12] So then, each of us will give an account of ourselves to God.
>
> ROMANS 14:7–10, 12

6. You don't know when your life will end, but you do know that one day you will give an account of that life to God. When you stand before the Lord, what do you want him to say? What are you doing to be a "good and faithful servant" to him (Matthew 25:21)?

STUDY 2

IN OUR FATHER'S HANDS

The story is told of a father who was crossing a bridge with his daughter. The region had recently seen a lot of rain, and the normally quiet stream below had swelled to a raging river. Concerned his daughter would be afraid, he asked her to hold his hand.

"No, Daddy," she replied. "*You* hold *my* hand."

When the father asked why, the girl explained that if she held his hand, she might let go. But if her father held her hand—well, she knew that he would *never* let go. She had complete trust that her father's grasp was firm and secure.

God does the same for us. Whether we recognize it or not, he walks with us as we go about the tasks of each day. Each time we take a risk, he is there. Each time we step out in faith, he is there. Each time we make a mistake, he is there. Each time we work through worry or anxiety or stress or anger or doubt—he is right there beside us, holding our hand.

As we have seen, there were many times when God sent Elijah into enemy territory. He told Elijah to announce the drought to Ahab. He sent Elijah back to Ahab when the drought was ending. He instructed Elijah to confront Ahab after the killing of Naboth. He then sent Elijah to Ahaziah to prophesy against him. Each time, Elijah was taking a risk. But each time, he went in confidence because he knew his life was in the Lord's hands.

That's the important part, by the way. *He* is holding on to us, not the other way around. Even when Elijah fled to Horeb and hid under a broom bush, the Lord was with him. We, likewise, don't have to maintain spiritual perfection in order to qualify ourselves for his presence. We don't have to be the ones who reach out to him and hold on to him with our strength and our resources. It's the other way around. Even when we mess up, he holds on to us. This means the best thing we can do is learn to trust his grasp at all times.

Best of all, we can trust that our heavenly Father will hold us as we come to the end of our lives. As the psalmist wrote, "For this is God, our God forever and ever; He will be our guide even to death" (Psalm 48:14 NKJV). King David added, "Yea, though I walk through the valley of the shadow of death, I will fear no evil; for You are with me" (23:4 NKJV).

There will come a time when we'll let go of this world. But we don't have to be afraid of that moment. We can trust that our loving heavenly Father will hold us by the hand—and never let us go.

1. Think about some of the key moments over the course of your life when you knew that God was with you. These could be trials you faced, or obstacles you overcame, or successes you achieved. First, write down what happened in these moments.

Time Period	What Key Moment Happened During This Time?
During childhood	
As a teen	
As a young adult	
In the past ten years	
Today	

2. Now write down how you knew that God was present and with you in each moment. How did you recognize that he was "holding your hand" during this time?

Specific Moment	How Did You Know That God Was with You?
During childhood	
As a teen	
As a young adult	
In the past ten years	
Today	

When it comes to your departure from this life into the next, be assured, God has you by the hand. Do not allow the fear of death to rob joy from your life. "[Jesus] died to rescue all of us who live each day in fear of dying" (Hebrews 2:15 CEV).

Let's remain alert and steadfast, knowing that at any moment we will be "caught up in the clouds to meet the Lord in the air" (1 Thessalonians 4:17 NLT).

Let's live with Elijah-level courage and confidence. He knew that his last day was upon him, yet he lived it as he had lived countless prior days. He simply went about his work and waited on his Lord. When Christ comes, may we be found earnestly doing the work we've been given to do.[32]

3. Take another look at 1 Kings 19:1–9. Remember that even the prophet Elijah gave in to fear at times—even asking the Lord to take his life in this situation! How did God instead reassure Elijah that he *held* the prophet's life in his hands? What encouragement does this give you that God will be present and with you in your fears?

4. The primary theme of this study is how to develop unbreakable courage in the Christian life. Why is courage necessary to maintain a proper view of death and dying?

5. On a practical level, what does it look like to "remain alert and steadfast" as a follower of Jesus? How might that help you to confront the fear of death?

> 4 Rejoice in the Lord always. I will say it again: Rejoice! 5 Let your gentleness be evident to all. The Lord is near. 6 Do not be anxious about anything, but in every situation, by prayer and petition, with thanksgiving, present your requests to God. 7 And the peace of God, which transcends all understanding, will guard your hearts and your minds in Christ Jesus.
>
> PHILIPPIANS 4:4-7

6. Take a moment to underline all the commands given in this passage. Which of those applies to choosing faith over fear as you contemplate the end of your life?

STUDY 3

THE GOD OF ISRAEL LIVES!

Do you remember *Jaws*? The movie told a fictional story of a monster shark making a meal out of the swimmers off the New England coastline. One iconic scene involved a crusty boat captain, the police chief, and a scientist. They set off on the captain's fishing boat in search of the shark. When they found it, they nearly fell over in fright. The chief delivered one of the most famous lines in cinema history: "You're gonna need a bigger boat!"

But suppose those three men had been riding in a larger vessel. Suppose they were standing on the deck of USS *Missouri*. Launched in 1944, it was the largest US battleship ever commissioned. "Mighty Mo," as it was called, was 887 feet in length and 108 feet in width.[33] Had the three men seen the giant shark from the deck of that warship, they would have reacted differently. They would have noticed the shark and maybe taken pictures of it. But would they have feared it? No.

The sea of life is swimming with sharks. They attack, gouge, and devour. But they cannot destroy you. Why? Because you are on the vessel called USS *Living God*. You are safe in his hands, established in his plans, and sustained in his grace.

Remember how Elijah burst onto the scene of Scripture: "Elijah the Tishbite, of the inhabitants of Gilead, said to Ahab, 'As the LORD God of Israel lives, before whom I stand, there shall not be dew nor rain these years, except at my word'" (1 Kings 17:1 NKJV).

The rain wasn't the important part of that proclamation. Neither was Elijah's heritage as a Tishbite or his homeland of Gilead. No, the main attraction was that morsel in the middle: "The LORD God of Israel lives."

This is the core message of Elijah's story. It was the source of his unbreakable courage. The Lord our God lives! More than that, he is the One on whom we stand. He is not distant, off pruning faraway galaxies while we suffer here on earth. No, our heavenly Father is as close as a heartbeat and solid as the stone beneath our feet.

In many ways, this is the central question of your life today. Right this moment. Do you believe that your God lives? Do you live as if he is close to you and desires to know you? Do you work as if your actions echo for eternity?

1. The fact that you serve a *living* God is a theme repeated throughout the Bible. Look up the following passages and write down what each says about the God you serve.

Passage	What This Says About God
Psalm 18:46	
Isaiah 45:5	
Jeremiah 10:10	
1 Thessalonians 1:8–10	
Revelation 21:3	

2. Look again at Elijah's first words in the Bible in 1 Kings 17:1. Remember that he lived in a culture that viewed the Canaanites gods Baal and Asherah as being alive, powerful, and active. Given this context, why did Elijah stress that he served a *living* god?

9 When they had crossed, Elijah said to Elisha, "Tell me, what can I do for you before I am taken from you?"

"Let me inherit a double portion of your spirit," Elisha replied.

10 "You have asked a difficult thing," Elijah said, "yet if you see me when I am taken from you, it will be yours—otherwise, it will not."

11 As they were walking along and talking together, suddenly a chariot of fire and horses of fire appeared and separated the two of them, and Elijah went up to heaven in a whirlwind. 12 Elisha saw this and cried out, "My father! My father! The chariots and horsemen of Israel!" And Elisha saw him no more. Then he took hold of his garment and tore it in two.

13 Elisha then picked up Elijah's cloak that had fallen from him and went back and stood on the bank of the Jordan. 14 He took the cloak that had fallen from Elijah and struck the water with it. "Where now is the LORD, the God of Elijah?" he asked. When he struck the water, it divided to the right and to the left, and he crossed over.

2 KINGS 2:9-14

3. Elijah also wanted Elisha to understand that he served a *living* God. It was beyond Elijah's power to grant Elisha a double portion of his spirit. However, if *God* allowed Elisha to see him taken into heaven, it would indicate his request had been granted.[34] Why was it important for Elisha to receive the answer to his request directly from God?

4. Notice what Elisha said after seeing Elijah taken up into heaven and then picking up his cloak: "Where now is the LORD, the God of Elijah?" (verse 14). Why do you think Elisha asked this question? How did the Lord answer his question?

> The cynic looks at the confusion and chaos of the world and feels hopeless, angry, and fearful. The believer looks at the confusion and chaos and feels empowered and beloved. *The God of Israel lives!* It's all a matter of faith.[35]

5. Read Jeremiah 17:7–8. The believer looks at the chaos of this world but "does not fear when heat comes." How has your understanding of biblical courage changed or grown as you have worked through Elijah's story in this study?

6. Consider the closing questions from the devotional reading above: *Do you believe that your God lives? Do you live as if he is close to you and desires to know you? Do you work as if your actions echo for eternity?* What are your answers to those questions?

WRAP UP

Connect with a fellow group member and discuss some of the key insights from this session. Use any of the following prompts to help guide your discussion.

- What have you enjoyed most about this study? What most inspired you and challenged you as you went through the material?
- What are some of the fears you uncovered when you thought about your own death? How has God helped you with those fears this week?
- What are some of the moments you identified in your life when God made his presence known to you? What impact did that have on you?
- What steps are you taking to imitate Elijah and Jesus as they worked, served, and ministered during the final seasons of their lives?
- What is something big, bold, and courageous that you want to accomplish for God? What is standing in your way?

Use this time to go back and complete any of the study and reflection questions from previous days that you weren't able to finish. Make note of what God has revealed to you in these days. Finally, talk with your group about what study you may want to go through next. Put a date on the calendar for when you'll meet next to study God's Word and dive deeper into community.

LEADER'S GUIDE

Thank you for leading your group through this study! What you are doing is valuable and will make a difference in the lives of others. *Unbreakable Courage* is a six-session Bible study built around video content and small-group interaction. As the group leader, picture yourself as the host of a party. Your job is to manage the details so that when your guests arrive, they can focus on one another and on the interaction around the topic for that session.

Your role as the group leader is not to answer all the questions or reteach the content—the video, book, and study guide will do most of that work. Your job is to guide the experience and cultivate your small group into a connected and engaged community. This will make it a place for members to process, question, and reflect. There are several elements in this leader's guide that will help you as you structure your study and reflection time, so be sure to follow along and take advantage of each one.

BEFORE YOU BEGIN

Before your first meeting, make sure the group members have a copy of this study guide. You can also hand out the study guides at your first meeting and give the members time to look over the material and ask any preliminary questions. Also, make sure that the group members are aware they have access to the streaming videos at any time by following the instructions provided with this guide. During your first meeting, ask the members to provide their names, phone numbers, and email addresses so that you can keep in touch.

Generally, the ideal size for a group is eight to ten people, which will ensure that everyone has enough time to participate in discussions. If you have more people, break up the main group into smaller subgroups. Encourage those who show up at the first meeting to commit to attending for the duration of the study, as this will help the group members get to know one another, create stability for the group, and help you know how best to prepare to lead the participants through the material.

Each session begins with an opening reflection in the Welcome section. The questions that follow in the Connect section serve as icebreakers to get the group members thinking about the topic. In the rest of the study, it's generally not a good idea to have everyone answer every question—a free-flowing discussion is more desirable. But with the icebreaker questions, you can go around the circle and ask each person to respond. Encourage shy people to share, but don't force them.

At your first meeting, let the group members know that each session also contains a personal study section they can use to continue to engage with the content until the next meeting. While doing this section is optional, it will help them cement the concepts presented during the group study time and help them better understand Elijah's story.

Let them know that if they choose to do so, they can watch the video for the next session by accessing the streaming code provided with this study guide. Invite them to bring any questions and insights to your next meeting, especially if they had a breakthrough moment or didn't understand something.

PREPARATION FOR EACH SESSION

As the leader, there are a few things you should do to best prepare for each meeting:

- **Read through the session.** This will help you become more familiar with the content and know how to structure the discussion times.
- **Decide how the videos will be used.** Determine whether you want the members to watch the videos ahead of time (again, via the streaming access code provided with this study guide) or together as a group.
- **Decide which questions you want to discuss.** Based on the length of your group discussions, you may not be able to get through all the questions. So look over the discussion questions and mark which ones you definitely want to cover.
- **Be familiar with the questions you want to discuss.** When the group meets, you'll be watching the clock, so be familiar with the questions you've selected.
- **Pray for your group.** Pray for your group members and ask God to lead them as they study his Word and listen to his Spirit.

Remember, in many cases, there will be no one "right" answer to the questions. Answers will vary, especially when the group members are sharing their personal experiences.

STRUCTURING THE DISCUSSION TIME

You will need to determine how long you want your meetings to last so you can plan your time accordingly. Suggested times for each section have been provided in this study guide, and if you adhere to these times, your group will meet for ninety minutes. However, many groups like to meet for two hours. If this describes your particular group, follow the times listed in the right-hand column of the chart given below.

Section	90 Minutes	120 Minutes
CONNECT (discuss one or more of the opening questions for the session)	15 minutes	20 minutes
WATCH (watch the teaching material together and take notes)	20 minutes	20 minutes
DISCUSS (discuss the study questions you selected ahead of time)	35 minutes	50 minutes
RESPOND (write down key takeaways)	10 minutes	15 minutes
CLOSE (pray together and dismiss)	10 minutes	15 minutes

As the group leader, it is up to you to keep track of the time and to keep things on schedule. You might want to set a timer for each segment so that both you and the group members know when the time is up. (There are some good phone apps for timers that play a gentle chime or other pleasant sound instead of a disruptive noise.)

Don't be concerned if group members are quiet or slow to share. People are often quiet when they are pulling together ideas, and this might be a new experience for them. Just ask a question and let it hang in the air until someone shares. You can then say, "Thank you. What about others? What came to you when you watched that portion of the teaching?"

GROUP DYNAMICS

Leading a group through *Unbreakable Courage* will prove to be highly rewarding both to you and your group members. But you still may encounter challenges along the way! Discussions can get off track. Group members may not be sensitive to the needs and ideas of others. Some might worry that they will be expected to talk about matters that make them feel awkward. Others may express comments that result in disagreements.

To help ease this strain on you and the group, consider the following ground rules:

- When someone raises a question or comment that is off the main topic, suggest you deal with it another time, or, if you feel led to go in that direction, let the group know you will be spending some time discussing it.

- If someone asks a question that you don't know how to answer, admit it and move on. At your discretion, feel free to invite group members to comment on questions that call for personal experience.

- If you find that one or two people are dominating the discussion time, direct a few questions to others in the group. Outside the main group time, ask the more dominating members to help you draw out the quieter ones. Work to make them part of the solution instead of part of the problem.

- When a disagreement occurs, encourage the group members to process the matter in love. Encourage those on opposite sides to restate what they heard the other side say about the matter, and then invite each side to evaluate if that perception is accurate. Lead the group in examining other passages related to the topic and look for common ground.

When any of these issues arise, encourage your group members to follow these words from Scripture: "Love one another" (John 13:34); "If it is possible, as far as it depends on you, live at peace with everyone" (Romans 12:18); "Whatever is true . . . noble . . . right . . . pure . . . lovely . . . if anything is excellent or praiseworthy—think about such things" (Philippians 4:8); and, "Everyone should be quick to listen, slow to speak and slow to become angry" (James 1:19). This will make your group time more rewarding and beneficial for everyone who attends.

Thank you again for leading your group. You are making a difference in your members' lives and having an impact on their journey toward a better understanding of what it means to follow in the footsteps of Elijah and live for God with *unbreakable courage.*

NOTES

1. This is a famous rallying cry from William Shakespeare's *Henry V* (act 3, scene 1).
2. Max Lucado, *Unbreakable Courage: Strong Faith in an Age of Anxiety, Chaos, and Exhaustion* (Thomas Nelson, 2026), 11–12.
3. Lucado, *Unbreakable Courage*, 21.
4. Rick Atchley, *The Life of Elijah*, part 3.
5. Jon Rivers, host, *20 the Countdown Magazine*, podcast, "Rich Mullins Radio Special," October 1, 2017, https://podcast.20thecountdown.com/episodes/rich-mullins-radio-special.
6. Lucado, *Unbreakable Courage*, 24–25.
7. Aïcha Rahmouni, *Divine Epithets in the Ugaritic Alphabetic Texts* (Brill, 2008), 84.
8. *Merriam-Webster Dictionary*, "faith," www.merriam-webster.com/dictionary/faith.
9. Lucado, *Unbreakable Courage*, 39.
10. Lucado, *Unbreakable Courage*, 48–49.
11. Lucado, *Unbreakable Courage*, 50–51.
12. Lucado, *Unbreakable Courage*, 57–58.
13. Lucado, *Unbreakable Courage*, 61–62.
14. "Fertility Cults of Canaan," *That the World May Know*, www.thattheworldmayknow.com/fertility-cults-of-canaan.
15. *Oxford English Dictionary*, "justice," www.oed.com/dictionary/justice_n.
16. Tim Keller, "Justice in the Bible," Gospel in Life, https://quarterly.gospelinlife.com/justice-in-the-bible.
17. "How Dangerous Is Lightning?" National Weather Service, www.weather.gov/safety/lightning-odds.
18. "Most Lightning Strikes Survived," *Guiness World Records*, www.guinnessworldrecords.com/world-records/most-lightning-strikes-survived.
19. C. S. Lewis, *Mere Christianity* (Harper San Francisco, 2001).
20. Lucado, *Unbreakable Courage*, 91.
21. Lucado, *Unbreakable Courage*, 101–102.
22. Lucado, *Unbreakable Courage*, 109.
23. Lucado, *Unbreakable Courage*, 110.
24. *David Blaine: Do Not Attempt,* episode 2, "SE Asia," 2025.
25. Lucado, *Unbreakable Courage*, 114–115
26. Lucado, *Unbreakable Courage*, 126–127.
27. Lucado, *Unbreakable Courage*, 131–132.
28. Charles Spurgeon, *Morning and Evening* (Crossway, 2025).
29. Mark Twain, *The Adventures of Huckleberry Finn* (Reader's Library Classics, 2022).
30. Eric Metaxas, *Bonhoeffer: Pastor, Martyr, Prophet, Spy* (Thomas Nelson, 2010), 528.
31. Lucado, *Unbreakable Courage*, 144–145.
32. Lucado, *Unbreakable Courage*, 150.
33. "Ship Characteristics," Battleship Missouri Memorial, https://ussmissouri.org/history/the-ship/ship-characteristics.
34. Richard D. Patterson and Hermann J. Austel, "1, 2 Kings," in *The Expositor's Bible Commentary*, ed. Tremper Longman III and David E. Garland, vol. 3, *1 Samuel–2 Kings* (Zondervan Academic, 2009), 813.
35. Lucado, *Unbreakable Courage*, 157.

ABOUT MAX LUCADO

Photography by Amanda Mae Steele

Since entering the ministry in 1978, Max Lucado has served churches in Miami, Florida; Rio de Janeiro, Brazil; and San Antonio, Texas. He currently serves as the teaching minister of Oak Hills Church in San Antonio. He is the recipient of the 2021 ECPA Pinnacle Award for his outstanding contribution to the publishing industry and society at large. He is America's best-selling inspirational author with more than 150 million products in print.

Visit his website at MaxLucado.com.
Join the Max Lucado Community:
Facebook.com/MaxLucado
Instagram.com/MaxLucado
X.com/MaxLucado
YouTube.com/MaxLucadoOfficial